A POSTCARD
FROM THE
DEE

Jan Dobrzynski

The
History
Press

To Peter Pears

First published 2009

The History Press
The Mill, Brimscombe Port
Stroud, Gloucestershire, GL5 2QG
www.thehistorypress.co.uk

© Jan Dobrzynski, 2009

The right of Jan Dobrzynski to be identified as the Author
of this work has been asserted in accordance with the
Copyrights, Designs and Patents Act 1988.

British Library Cataloguing in Publication Data.
A catalogue record for this book is available from the British Library.

ISBN 978 0 7509 5119 7

Typesetting and origination by The History Press
Printed in Great Britain

Contents

'Connected with the Dee there is a wonderful Druidical legend to the following effect. The Dee springs from two fountains high up in Merionethshire, called Dwy Fawr and Dwy Fach, or the great and little Dwy, whose waters pass through those of Lake Bala without mingling with them, and come out at its northern extremity. These fountains had their names from two individuals, Dwy Fawr and Dwy Fach, who escaped from the Deluge, when all the rest of the human race were drowned, and the passing of the waters of the two fountains through the lake, without being confounded with its flood, is emblematic of the salvation of the two individuals from the Deluge, of which the lake is a type'.

(*Wild Wales*, George Borrow, 1857)

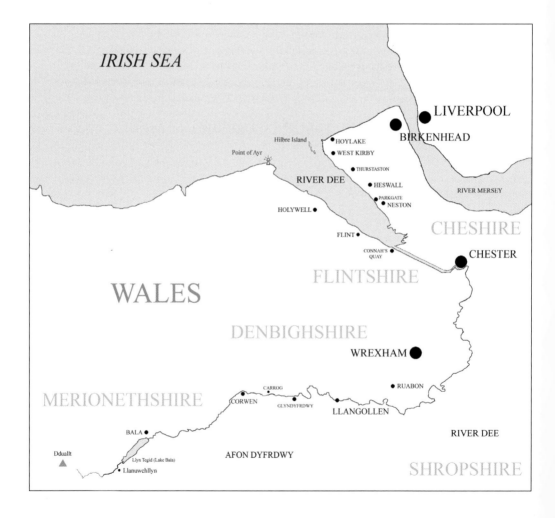

Introduction

By the end of the nineteenth century, the postcard and especially the picture postcard had become an integral part of the postal system in Britain. It was by far the most expedient means of communication, short of talking or meeting people face to face. The collection, distribution and delivery of mail, helped by the improved roads and railways, reached new standards of speed and efficiency, so much so, that practically every town and village had a regular daily postal service, and some had several deliveries throughout the day.

By the first decade of the twentieth century, the postcard had become the cheapest and most widespread means of sending a message, probably analogous to today's phone texts. In the towns and cities, it was possible to post a card with a message, and receive an answer within a day. In some instances it was possible to send a postcard in the morning receive a reply by return at the end of the morning, and send a further card and still expect an answer by the final post in the afternoon. The earliest postcards appeared in the 1870s and started out as plain cards; one side was used for writing a message and the other for the postal address. Only the post office was allowed to issue these cards, which came with the stamp already printed on the front. This type of card proved very popular and eventually privately owned cards appeared from 1872 (breaking the post office monopoly), while further legislation in the 1890s permitted privately printed cards and picture postcards with adhesive stamps to be sent by the postal system. By 1899 the regulations were further amended to permit private cards up to a maximum size of 5½ x 3½ in to be sent. From that time onwards, the picture postcard gained massive acceptance and the postcard photographer and illustrator began to cover every county, town, village, event and activity.

The postcard was a cherished possession and hundreds of millions were printed each year during their golden age between 1902 and 1914; some were posted, others found their way into collectors' albums from the outset, to be kept as souvenirs and keepsakes of places visited or dreamt about. Many of these old cards survive to the present day and are enthusiastically collected and sought-after by collectors and historians. The picture postcards in this book date back to the early years of the twentieth century. They show the River Dee as it once appeared to earlier generations of artists and photographers. The views capture halcyon days on the river, the picturesque countryside and coast, and include cities, towns, and villages.

Not to be confused with the two other rivers called Dee that are both in Scotland, the River Dee Aberdeenshire and the River Dee Galloway, this book, illustrated with over 200 old postcards, describes the river known to the Romans as Deva and to the Welsh as Dyfrdwy. The Dee rises in the ancient mountains of Snowdonia on the slopes of the hillside called Dduallt, high above the village of Llanuwchllyn. The Dyfrdwy's vigorous and youthful flow soon wanes as it is absorbed into the broad reaches of Wales's most beautiful and natural expanse of water, Lake Bala (Llyn Tegid). The lake is a magnet to visitors with sailing, camping or walking in mind. Whether the visitor stays a day, a weekend or longer they are sure to experience the charm and serenity of this lake. There are plenty of campsites, hotels and B&B establishments, which cater for visitors to the local countryside or the nearby town of Bala (which naturally takes its name from the lake). About a hundred years ago, when earlier generations of visitors came to visit and stay, they would arrive on the railways from the industrial Midlands, Cheshire and Lancashire keen to enjoy the delights of the country. Most were mindful to tell their friends and family that they had arrived safely, and how much 'they wished that they were here.'

What better way to say it than to write the sentiment on a postcard and send it off in the full knowledge that the card was likely to arrive the following day. There was also no better way to show those that one 'wished were here' where here was – the picture postcard often showed the hotel, the boarding house, hotel, street and even the railway station at the destination.

The Dee emerges from Lake Bala with new vigour, a full-grown river, flowing in a north-easterly direction swelled by countless streams and the rivers including the Afon Tryweryn, Afon Ceidiog and Afon Alwen. The Afon Dyfrdwy flows in an easterly direction at Corwen, the next largest town on the river. The town and district are strongly associated with Owain Glyndwr (1349–1416), lord of Glyn Dyfrdwy, a Welsh prince and symbol of Welsh nationalism. After flowing through the villages of Carrog and Glyndyfrdwy, the river cuts its way into the Vale of Llangollen closely paralleled by road, canal and railway which use the valley floor as a natural route through the steep Welsh hills. At Plas Berwyn the road, railway and the canal (that takes its water from the Dyfrdwy, cascading over the Horseshoe Falls) all meet at the narrow entrance to the vale.

The town of Llangollen stands astride the river surrounded by steep hills in every direction. It is famous for its International Eisteddfod and also Plas Newydd, the former home of the Ladies of Llangollen, who held court to the rich and famous in the early years of the nineteenth century. The house was latterly headquarters to the indefatigable George Borrow for his excursions into *Wild Wales*. Other attractions nearby include the Horseshoe Pass and the romantic ruins of Valle Crucis Abbey, Castell Dinas Bran and the engineering wonders of the Llangollen branch of the Shropshire Union Canal. The Dyfrdwy is crossed by Offa's Dyke and flows under Telford's magnificent aqueduct at Pontcysyllte, which carries the Llangollen Canal high above the river valley. The Afon Dyfrdwy is then joined by the Afon Ceiriog, which is also crossed by the Llangollen Canal by an equally spectacular aqueduct at Chirk.

The Dee as it is now known, crosses into England and for a time briefly forms the border between Shropshire and Wrexham (formerly part of Denbighshire). It then enters the county of Cheshire were it meanders through the low-lying Cheshire plain before reaching the historic city of Chester. The city of Chester was founded on the Roman fortress of Deva, once home to the XX legion (Legio XX Valeria Victrix). A perfect medieval wall – which incorporates part of the Roman defences punctuated by gates and towers – surrounds Chester. The city boasts numerous attractions: half-timbered buildings complete with rows, a cathedral, a castle, a racecourse, public parks and beautiful open spaces.

Tamed of meandering and confined to an artificial channel, this 'canalised' length of the Dee flows in a straight line for 5 miles to Hawarden Bridge. Beyond are the industries around Shotton and Connah's Quay. Just 2 miles further on, the Dee emerges in a partially silted estuary, which is a haven for wildlife and a birdwatchers' paradise, which forms the natural boundary between Wales and England. The Wirral peninsula and the towns of Neston, Heswall, West Kirby and Hoylake form the eastern shore while the towns of Flint and Holywell lie on the Welsh western shore of the Dee estuary. The disused lighthouse at the Point of Ayr on the tip of North Wales and the sandstone outcrops at Hoylake and the rocky islands at Hilbre on the Wirral, mark the final reaches of the river.

Unlike the Severn or Wye, a long-distance footpath does not accompany the Dee on its journey to Liverpool Bay and the Irish Sea, though a number of public paths and cycle ways join it at various reaches. Details of these are given at the appropriate points in the text.

All the postcards included in this book are from the author's own collection. Publication details are given at the end of the captions, if and as they appear on the cards.

Details of the course of footpaths or cycle ways close to the Dee are given at the beginning of each chapter and after the captions as appropriate

1

A Welsh River

'I turned up a street, which lead to the east, and soon found myself beside the lake at the north-west extremity of which Bala stands. It appeared a very noble sheet of water stretching from north to south for several miles.'

(*Wild Wales*, George Borrow, 1857)

The Dee has no long-distance footpath following its entire length unlike the other two great rivers that flow through Wales and England – the Severn and Wye. However, on its journey through Wales from Lake Bala (which in Welsh means 'the efflux of a river from a lake') onwards, roads closely follow the course of the river on both sides of the valley, and the Bala Lake Railway runs alongside the southern shore of the lake. A preserved railway meets the river at Llangollen and many local paths follow its course for parts of its journey to the sea.

(Photomatic Ltd)

The Afon Dyfrdwy (before it adopts its English name the River Dee) springs from the steep eastern slopes of Dduallt (Black Hill in Welsh), 4 miles west of the small village of Llanuwchllyn through which it flows as a sizeable stream. *(Park & Son, Newton, Posted 1917)*

Mountains, lakes and rivers were a popular theme for the postcard illustrator; this romanticised view shows Wales's largest natural lake, Llyn Tegid (Lake Bala), with the Cambrian Mountains as a backdrop. The Afon Dyfrdwy flows into the lake from the south. A tale based on local superstition suggests that the waters of river and lake never mix, and that the Afon Dyfrdwy flows through the lake as a separate current. *(Raphael Tuck & Sons, 'Art' Series, Posted 1910)*

Llyn Tegid stretches into the distance over 4 miles long, and a mile wide *(Valentine & Sons, Ltd, Dundee & London)*

A once-common rural scene from the early years of the twentieth century, sheaves bundled and tied, ripening on the western hillside above Llyn Tegid, and Bala, the town named after the exit of the river from the lake. On these steep hillsides it was usual for the scythe man to cut round the edges of fields to make a start for the horse-drawn reaper and binder. The wooden rake would suggest that the crop was gathered and sheaved by hand. *(Frith's Series, F. Frith & Co., Reigate)*

The Town of Bala seen from the south-west with a glimpse of the Afon Dyfrdwy (Dee) and the Bala &
Dolgelly (Dolgellau) Railway behind the trees in the foreground (the lake is just out of view on the left of
the picture). In the distance are the spires of Christ Church and the English Chapel, further beyond them
the Tower of Bala College. *(Valentine & Sons, Dundee & London)*

In 1804, sixteen-year-old Mary Jones walked 25 miles bare foot from Llanfihangel y Pennant to
Bala to collect a bible from the Methodist clergyman Thomas Charles. Since he had no stock left, and
moved by her distress, he gave her his own; this incident prompted him to edit the bible in Welsh and
ultimately contributed to the formation of the Great British & Foreign Bible Society. A statue of the Revd
Thomas Charles (1755–1814) stands in Tegid Street next to the chapel; his grandson, the Revd David
Charles (1812–78) and the Revd Lewis Edwards (1809–87) who was married to Thomas Charles's
granddaughter opened the Bala Calvinistic Methodist College for men in 1867, which later became the
theological college for North Wales. Coleg y Bala, the Welsh title it is known by today, is a youth centre
owned by the Presbyterian Church of Wales. *(Photochrom Co. Ltd, posted 1906)*

Bala, High Street.

Bala's High Street was wide enough to hold a market for the sale of goods and produce, which in the eighteenth century included locally manufactured flannel, stockings, gloves and hosiery. Square courts and side streets lead off from the main thoroughfare. The layout of the streets dates from the fourteenth century, after Roger de Mortimer founded the town. Tomen y Bala is the remains of a motte and bailey fortification dating from that time. This quiet scene in the late 1930s is untypical even for the time; nowadays the high street shops, pubs and restaurants attract thousands of summer visitors eager to enjoy the lake and the water sports amenities. *(F. Frith & Co., Reigate, posted 1937)*

This advertisement for the Plascoch Hotel seen on the right-hand side of the photograph above proclaims how families, tourists and commercial gentleman will find every comfort. *(Gossiping Guide to Wales, 1877 edition)*

Bala.

PLASCOCH HOTEL,

BALA.

FAMILIES, TOURISTS, and COMMERCIAL GENTLEMEN will find every comfort at above Hotel.

CHARGES MODERATE.

SPACIOUS BILLIARD ROOM.

Boat on the Lake, for the use of Visitors to this Hotel.

Coaches to and from the Station.

DAVIES, Proprietors.

46519. BALA: HIGH STREET, ELLIS STATUE.

White Lion Royal Hotel, Bala

Opposite, top: Thomas Edward Ellis (1859–99) is another famous son, a Welsh politician and leader of Cymru Fydd, the movement for home rule for Wales. Ellis called for a legislative assembly for Wales. A Liberal MP for Merionethshire and Chief Liberal Whip, four years after his death a bronze statue in the High Street was unveiled to commemorate him. *(Photochrom Co. Ltd, Wedgwood Series, posted 1913)*

Opposite, bottom: The White Lion Royal Hotel is a posting and coaching inn which dates back to 1759. The 'Royal' part was added after the visit of Queen Victoria, who was reputed to have remarked about how modern the sanitary engineering was – the hotel had a fitted inside toilet. On his travels through Wales, George Borrow also visited the hotel – in fact on two separate occasions. When served home-brewed beer by Tom Jenkins the waiter, Borrow wrote, 'I tasted it, and then took a copious draught. The ale was indeed, admirable, equal to the best that I had ever before drunk – rich and mellow, with scarcely any smack of hop in it, and though so pale and delicate to the eye, nearly as strong as brandy.' Also remarking about breakfast, 'A noble breakfast it was; such indeed, as I might have read of, but had never before seen. There was tea and coffee, a goodly white loaf and butter; there were a couple of eggs and mutton chops. There was broiled and pickled salmon – there was fried trout – There were also potted trout and potted shrimps. Mercy upon me! I have never previously seen such a breakfast set before me nor indeed have I subsequently. Yes I have subsequently, and at that very house when I visited it some month after.' The hotel, extensively refurbished but still recognisable from this postcard, offers the same high standards of service to its modern guests. *(Valentine Series, posted 1909)*

(Gossiping Guide to Wales, 1877 edition)

Looking north-west onto Llyn Tegid's east shore and the A494 road skirting the lakeside. In the distance is Pont Mwnwgl y Llyn, the Dee Bridge and the edge of the Promenade. *(F. Frith & Co., Reigate, posted 1951)*

The A494 lake road heading south-east with the Aran Mountains to the south of Llyn Tegid. In the range there are no fewer than fourteen summits above 2,000ft including Aran Fawddwy at 2,969ft and Aran Benllyn at 2,904ft. *(F. Frith & Co., Reigate, Frith's Series)*

The Promenade leading to the Dee Bridge. After asking a man at his gate the way to Bala, George Borrow crossed here on his second visit to the town. Borrow writes, 'I thanked him and sped onward, and in about half an hour saw houses, then a bridge, then a lake on my left which I recognised as Lake Bala. I skirted the end of it came to a street cheerfully lighted up, and in a minute more was in the White Lion Inn.' *(F. Frith & Co., Reigate, Frith's Series)*

Here is the bridge that George Borrow crossed; its Welsh name is Pont Mwnwgl y Llyn (the bridge at the neck of the lake). Here the Dyfrdwy emerges from Llyn Tegid. The old bridge still exists, although it was bypassed in 1954 by a new girder bridge built over a diverted and deeper channel of the River Dee, part of a water regulation scheme which had the added effect of lowering the waters of Llyn Tegid. The old bridge is still there but high and dry. Close by is the narrow-gauge Bala Lake Railway's Pen y Bont (Bridge Head) terminus. The line operates a seasonal lakeside service from Llanuwchllyn on part of the former GWR Bala & Dolgelly Railway, which opened in 1868 and closed in 1965. *(Edwards' Series)*

Part of the same water regulatory scheme described on the previous page, the Afon Tryweryn, a principle tributary of the Afon Dyfrdwy (Dee), joins just below the bridge. It includes a series of weirs and channels along its course to regulate flow, and is seen here looking quite placid as it passes through wooded banks by the town. *(F. Frith & Co., Reigate, Frith's Series)*

The village of Llandderfel is just a little over 3 miles away from Bala. It is situated on the northern bank of Afon Dyfrdwy (Dee) and its bridge was built in 1896, which is at the foot of the Berwyn Mountains. Traditionally the villagers were employed in flannel-weaving, agriculture and sheep-rearing on the nearby hillsides. The church, dedicated to the sixth-century St Derfel, dates back to Tudor times and has a carved screen and rood loft. *(D. Howel Davies, posted 1939)*

About 8 miles further downriver, the five-span stone Corwen Bridge, which carries the London–Holyhead road across the Afon Dyfrdwy (Dee). *(Pictorial Stationery Co., London, Peacock Autochrom, posted 1912)*

It is here that the Afon Dyfrdwy (Dee) meets the Vale of Edeirnion, sloping in from the right, as the river turns due east to meander towards the Vale of Llangollen. The Berwyn Mountains and the Cynwyd Forest rise to the left of the picture above Corwen and its bridge a mile away in the distance. *(G.A. Jones, Corwen)*

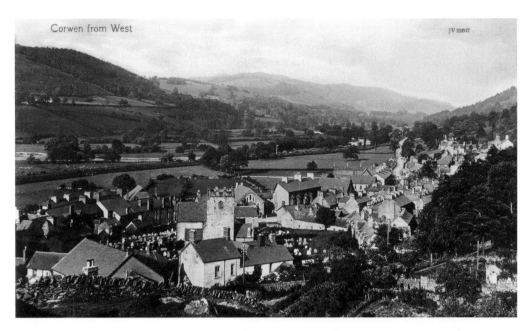

Corwen was an important stagecoach town and river crossing. The London–Holyhead Royal Mail and named stagecoaches 'Wonder' and 'Nimrod' from Shrewsbury used Corwen as a principle stopping-off point before the next towns, Betws-y-Coed, or Bala to the south on the Dolgellau route. The road and the railway follow the river west in this view, taken from Pen-y-Pigyn above the church dedicated to St Mael and St Sulien, which is seen in the centre of the picture. On the hillside slopes to the left is the ancient hill fort of Caer Drewyn. Written on the back of the card, 'Spent the night here not bad but very quiet, some good hills to go down.' *(Valentine & Sons Ltd, Dundee & London, posted)*

Again, from Pen-y-Pigyn, this time looking in a north-westerly direction onto the church and the town below. The GWR Ruabon & Dolgelly line forms the boundary between the town and the river meadows. *(Valentine & Sons Ltd, Dundee & London)*

A glimpse of Corwen station on the GWR Ruabon & Dolgelly (Dolgellau) line. The station served a junction between the GWR Ruabon & Dolgelly line and the London & North Western Denbigh, Ruthin & Corwen Railway (DR&C Rly). Behind the station and the town are the forested slopes of Pen-y-Pigyn and the Berwyn Hills. *(Unidentified, dated 1906)*

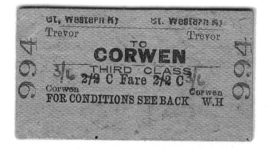

An assortment of railway tickets from local lines that inevitably paralleled the valley of the Dee and converged on Corwen. Trevor was a station in the Vale of Llangollen in between Ruabon and Llangollen. Bala was the town station on the Bala to Festiniog (Blaenau Ffestiniog) line that joined the GWR Ruabon & Dolgelly line at Bala Junction. The GWR rail tour ticket shows that Corwen was a popular holiday destination for tourists using the railway and local bus services. The final ticket is from the DR&C Rly line from Denbigh. *(Author's Collection)*

Victoria Bridge over the Afon Dyfrdwy (Dee). Two bridges once crossed here within the space of a few hundred yards; the other carried the DR&C Rly over the river. *(F. Frith & Co., Reigate, Frith's Series)*

Less than 3 miles further downriver from Victoria Bridge, another bridge crosses the Afon Dyfrdwy (Dee) at Carrog, a picturesque Welsh village famous for its association with Owain Glyndwr (*c.* 1349–1416), the figurehead of Welsh nationalism in the fifteenth century. The village is on the north bank of the river, centred on two chapels, a primary school and church. The Baptist chapel in the centre of the picture dates from 1896; it had been a Methodist chapel from 1872 and the local church from 1611, although it was greatly altered in the nineteenth century. This view is from the edge of the abandoned Penarth slate quarry and the Holyhead road, while further below is the Ruabon & Dolgelly Railway. In recent times, Carrog has seen the return of its railway and the current terminus of the Llangollen Steam Railway is at Pen-y-bont, although the railway preservation society is working its way inexorably towards Corwen. *(Unidentified, posted 1912)*

Looking towards the village from Carrog's five-span stone bridge, which dates from 1661. The listed structure crosses the Afon Dyfrdwy below the village, while to the right are elegant Victorian and Edwardian mansions, built as holiday homes for wealthy occupants from Liverpool and Manchester. *(Unidentified)*

The Afon Dyfrdwy (Dee) is closely followed for most of its journey to the sea by roads and railways. Both take advantage of the natural route scoured out by the river and the action of glaciers, thus avoiding the steep mountains and hills of the district. *(Unidentified, posted 1936)*

The Clwydian Way long-distance footpath leaves Carrog and the Ty Nant road at the edge of the village and climbs steeply towards Llantysilio Mountain

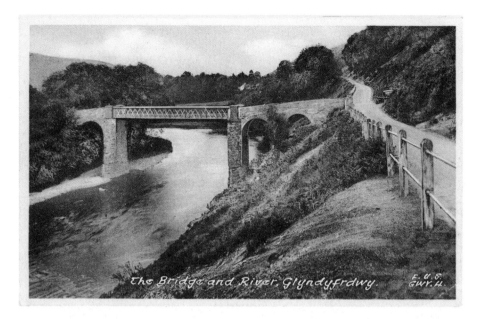

In 1400 at the manor of Glyndyfrdwy, Baron Owain Glyndwr proclaimed himself Prince of Wales, sparking off the rebellion against English rule. Alongside the modern A5 road stands an earth ringwork called Owain Glyndwr's Mount, built to guard the route through the Dee Valley, and in the valley below, a moat on the banks of Afon Dyfrdwy (Dee), which is thought to be the remains of Glyndwr's manor house. The bridge joins the Ty Nant road from the village of Carrog. To the right of the bridge are the slopes of Craig y Rhos. *(F. Frith & Co., Reigate, Frith's Series)*

Looking down from the A5 roadside, above the village of Glyndyfrdwy, the station and the railway line are visible on the right. Glyndyfrdwy is another stop on the preserved Llangollen Railway. On the opposite bank of the river are the group of houses called Rhosynwst and the crags of Craig y Rhos. *(Unidentified)*

This multi-view card shows Berwyn's famous attractions at the mouth of the Vale of Llangollen. The Berwyn range of hills is a large area of upland heath south of the Afon Dyfrdwy (Dee). *(Frith's Series, F. Frith & Co., Ltd, Reigate)*

Looking down from Bryniau-mawr Bank onto the tight bend of the river as it enters the Berwyn Vale. In the centre of the picture is the complex juxtaposition of road, railway and river bridges; below them is the Chain Bridge and the hotel named after it. *(Valentine's Bromotone, posted 1932)*

A ticket contemporary with the date of the postcard, issued by the GWR, a buff coloured pre-grouping ticket dated 27 April 1906. *(Courtesy John Hawkins' Collection)*

Kings Bridge carries a minor road (the B5103) across the Afon Dyfrdwy (Dee) at Berwyn. The road has to take a sharp curve past the railway station to leave the Holyhead road (A5). It then immediately dips downwards to clear the arches of the railway bridge that pass over it. *(Valentine's Series)*

Berwyn station and the Chain Bridge crossing the Afon Dyfrdwy (Dee) below. The station looks very much the same today, and this is still a favourite spot for rail enthusiasts to take photographs of steam trains leaving the station. The station opened with the Llangollen & Corwen Railway in 1865, and was taken over by the GWR in 1896. In 1954 it was renamed Berwyn Halt, but the station and the whole line were closed by British Railways in 1964 after flooding. The private Llangollen Railway reopened the station for steam-hauled services in 1982. *(The Wrench Series)*

THE HORSE SHOE PASS, LLANGOLLEN   11583

The road, which crosses the Afon Dyfrdwy at Berwyn, joins the Ruthin Road (A542) in the Afon Eglwyseg valley. After 3 miles, the A542 traverses the famous Horse Shoe Pass built in 1811, through Maesyrychen Mountain. Before the pass was built, the only way north was the drove route over Llantysilio Mountain or from Pentre-dwfr and the old pass at Bwlch yr Oernant. *(Salmon Series, Salmon Ltd, Sevenoaks)*

LGLN 109   VALLE CRUCIS ABBEY, LLANGOLLEN.   Copyright Frith's

Also in the Eglwyseg Valley are the remains of Valle Crucis Abbey, another famous attraction of the area. The abbey was founded in 1201 as a Cistercian house. Added to in subsequent centuries, it was dissolved by Royal Decree in 1537. The abbey ruins merge in perfectly with the green valley, hillside slopes and steep-sided mountains on the edge of Llangollen. *(Frith's Series, F. Frith & Co., Ltd Reigate)*

What remains of the abbey is remarkably well-preserved. The east end overlooks the monks' fishpond. *(Valentine's Series)*

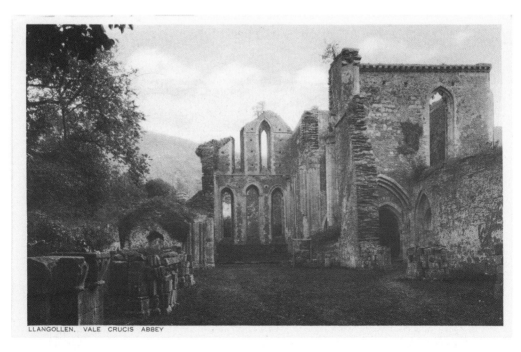

Looking east from inside the chapter house with a magnificent rib-vaulted roof on the right. *(Published by the Proprietor Hand Hotel, Llangollen The R.A.P. Co, London E.C.4)*

2

Through the Vale of Llangollen

'I was now in a wide valley – enormous hills were on my right. The road was good, and above it, in the side of a steep bank, was a causeway intended for foot passengers. It was overhung with hazel bushes. I walked along it to its termination, which was at Llangollen.'

(Wild Wales, George Borrow, 1857)

Llangollen takes its name from the church of Collen established by the seventh-century monk St Collen, who rode a white horse through the valley for one day to establish the boundaries of the parish. The Clwydian Way meets the Afon Dyfrdwy (Dee) at Corwen and Offa's Dyke crosses the river below the Pontcysyllte Aqueduct. The canal has a towpath to walk on and there are many hillside footpaths to explore Collen's parish.

(Vale Princess Series R. M. & S Ltd. S)

One of Llangollen's wonders is the Horseshoe Falls at Berwyn, built by Thomas Telford. The Afon Dyfrdwy (Dee) flows along the outer edge of the horseshoe, and 6 million gallons of water are channelled everyday into the head of a navigable feeder for the Llangollen Canal; the remaining flow of the river cascades over the horseshoe. The canal opened as a branch of the Ellesmere Canal Company (later the Shropshire Union Canal) in 1805. *(Unidentified)*

LLANGOLLEN. CHAIN BRIDGE   69735

The canal runs parallel to the Afon Dyfrdwy (Dee), and both river and canal pass under Kings Bridge (see page 24) and pass on opposite sides of the Chain Bridge Hotel. The hotel is named after the footbridge seen on the left, which crosses the river beside the hotel. An earlier chain bridge, built in 1814 by Exuperius Pickering, was used to carry coal and lime between the Llangollen Canal and the Holyhead road, and it was built over a much earlier crossing used by the monks of Valle Crucis Abbey. The bridge was strengthened on the instructions of Sir Henry Robertson, owner of Brymbo Steel Works. However, it was severely damaged during exceptionally bad floods in 1928, and the bridge was totally rebuilt in the following year. The Chain Bridge Hotel and Riverside Restaurant is still a popular spot for visitors directly opposite a spectacular waterfall and Berwyn station on the preserved Llangollen Steam Railway. *(Photochrom Co. Ltd, Tunbridge Wells)*

A little under a mile from the Horseshoe Falls the river drops rapidly down into the valley as the canal maintains practically the same level as where its waters originated. *(Silverette, Raphael Tuck & Sons, posted 1906)*

The Clwydian Way joins the canal towpath on its way through the town of Llangollen.

Picturesque canalside cottages on the outskirts of the town prompted the sender of this postcard, posted on 5 July 1912, to write, 'Percy and I are here for the day it is a lovely place to finish my holiday.' Thousands of visitors from around the world visit almost this same spot, as the Llangollen Royal International Pavilion just a few yards away from here, hosts the Llangollen International Musical Eisteddfod every year in July. *(Posted 1912, Frith's Series, F. Frith & Co. Ltd, Reigate)*

A particularly attractive wooded section of the canal next to the sluice gate and overflow above the Afon Dyfrdwy (Dee). This was a favourite spot for photographers and artists. *(Valentine's Series)*

It was the bearded Captain Jones (although captain was most likely an honorary title) who started the regular tourists' horse-drawn boat trips from Llangollen Wharf to the Horseshoe Falls in the early 1900s. Following on in the same tradition, forty-five-minute horse-drawn trips take visitors on the feeder canal, and two-hour trips on traditional narrow boats visit the Pontcysyllte Aqueduct. *(Valentine's Series)*

Looking down from Geraint – or alternatively named Barber's – Hill onto the predominantly nineteenth-century Llangollen that extends south-east of Bridge Street and Church Street. The less densely populated area is north of the bridge and includes the railway and the canal. *(Salmon Series, J. Salmon Ltd, Sevenoaks)*

LLANGOLLEN FROM PEN-Y-COED   11595

This time looking from Pen y Coed from the south-east with Geraint Hill rising up from the town on the left. Llangollen developed as an important staging town on the London to Holyhead road, which had been substantially improved over a period of fifteen years by Thomas Telford from 1815 onwards. On the left of the river is Llangollen's parish church and on the opposite bank is Lower Dee Mill flannel works. *(Gravure Style, Salmon Series, J. Salmon Ltd, Sevenoaks)*

A popular place to take a stroll is along the riverside Victoria Promenade which passes through well-tended gardens, tennis courts and a bowling green and from which there are views of the steam trains at Llangollen station, overlooked by Geraint Hill in the distance. *(Valentine's Series)*

Standing over the promenade is Glanrafon Evangelical Church, a Welsh Congregational chapel. *(R. M. & S. Ltd)*

The alternative name of Barbers's Hill for Moel y Geraint comes from the tale of Thomas Edwards, a schoolmaster who lived with his wife Maria at a cottage beside the Hand Hotel. In 1739, after a dispute with his wife over how to cook a leg of mutton, the schoolmaster threw a fit of rage and cut his wife's throat with a barber's razor. The schoolmaster was apprehended and sentenced to be hanged on a gibbet on the nearest hill overlooking the town. Geraint Hill was chosen and as he climbed the hill, he was given a final jug of ale from the landlady of the pub. He was then hanged at the top of the hill, and ever since the hill has been known as 'Moel y Barbwr', or 'Barber's Hill'. In the foreground is the millrace and weir of Llangollen watermill. *(Valentine's Series)*

The old cornmill at Dee Lane stands on the site of a much earlier mill founded by the monks of Valle Crucis Abbey. Rebuilt in 1786, it continued to mill corn up to 1895. For another eight decades it produced animal feed before finally closing in 1974. It is now a pub and restaurant. *(Frith's Series, F. Frith & Co. Ltd, Reigate, posted 1913)*

A sight seldom seen today: a coracle fisherman. Rod fishing is commonplace and is controlled by the Llangollen Angling Association which is responsible for 14 miles of fishing grounds on the river. The fishing is for salmon, trout, brown trout, rainbow trout and grayling. *(Glossy Photo Series, Griffith & Son, Castle Street, Llangollen)*

The road on the far right leads up to the Horseshoe Pass, and the Afon Dyfrdwy (Dee) is seen flowing under Llangollen Bridge and beside Llangollen railway station, which is built over a hefty retaining wall to protect it from the river. *(Celesque, Photochrom Co. Ltd, Tunbridge Wells)*

Llangollen station opened with the Vale of Llangollen Railway in 1861; the station was the terminus of the line from Ruabon for four years before the next section of line opened with the Llangollen & Corwen Railway to Llandrillo in 1865. After 1896, the railway was owned and operated by the GWR as far as Dolgellau, where it joined the Cambrian Railways line from Barmouth Junction (Morfa Mawddach). The whole route closed to passengers in 1965 and final closure was in 1968. In 1975, the Llangollen Railway Society rescued the station and line, and now runs regular steam train services to Carrog, with plans to extend the line to Corwen. *(Valentine's Series)*

Bishop John Trevor of Trevor Hall built the Dee Bridge in 1345, and today it is a scheduled ancient monument. A bridge has existed here since at least 1284 but the greater part of the present bridge probably dates from about 1500, with major repairs which took place in 1656, and the addition of another arch to cross the railway in 1861. The whole bridge was widened in the 1960s to accommodate increased road traffic. *(R.J. Smith)*

A view of the weir below the bridge and beside it the Royal Hotel, which was Llangollen's principle posting and coaching inn – it was originally known as the Kings Head. The Ladies of Llangollen and their distinguished guests often frequented the hotel. The hotel changed its name to commemorate the visit of Princess Victoria in 1832. *(Hugh Jones, Advertiser Office, Llangollen)*

THE ROYAL HOTEL,
LLANGOLLEN.

THE ABOVE FIRST-CLASS ESTABLISHMENT

Is beautifully situated on the Banks of the Dee, close to the far-famed Llangollen Bridge, and within three minutes' walk of the Railway Station, and has recently undergone great improvements and been refurnished with all modern conveniences.

SPACIOUS COFFEE ROOM,

With unequaled view of the neighbouring scenery and overlooking the River.

FREE FISHING ADJOINING THE HOTEL.

BILLIARD AND SMOKING ROOMS.   CROQUET LAWN.

Families Boarded by the Week.

POSTING IN ALL ITS BRANCHES.

THE HOTEL OMNIBUS MEETS ALL TRAINS.

C. JONES, Proprietress.

The hotel boasts its services to the visitor in this advertisement. *(Gossiping Guide to Wales, 1877)*

Two views of Castle Street. Firstly, from the south and the crossroads with Berwyn Street (the Holyhead road), the bridge is at the far end of the road. The view has not greatly changed, but the most noticeable difference today would be parked cars in front of the buildings. On the left is the Welsh Wesleyan Seion Chapel opened in 1903. *(Valentine's Series)*

A second view looking towards the Holyhead road from the crossroads at Parade Street and Bridge Street. On the right is the Market Hall which was built in 1867. The building comprised open arches on the ground floor, which were closed off and converted into shops. Next door to the Market Hall stands the 1860 chapel that housed a congregation of 400. After it closed in 1982 it was used as a council building and is currently a Tourist Information Centre. *(Unidentified)*

A night-time scene lit by moonlight: Llangollen with Castell Dinas Bran (Crow Castle) overlooking the town and the imposing escarpment of the Panorama Walk beyond it. *(Valentine's Series)*

The Panorama Walk is part of a ridge and outcrop of carboniferous limestone, which extends from Worlds End from the north through Eglwyseg and on to Trevor. The Panorama Walk rises at Trevor and follows the ridge overlooking Castle Dinas Bran, offering stunning views of the Shropshire and Cheshire plains. *(Valentine's)*

The Offa's Dyke Path follows the ridge and Panorama Walk before crossing the Afon Dyfrdwy at Cyslltau Bridge below Pontcysyllte.

THE CASTLE, LLANGOLLEN.

The ruins of Castell Dinas Bran is a lofty landmark high above Llangollen and visible from every part of the vale. It sits high on an isolated hill reached by a steep climb from the north of the town. From the top, the views of the Vale of Llangollen and the Dyfrdwy (Dee) Valley are stunning. *(Hugh Jones, Llangollen)*

Ruins, Castell Dinas Bran, Llangollen   42992

Castell Dinas Bran was built in the 1260s by Prince Gruffydd ap Madoc, the founder of Valle Crucis Abbey, to guard the strategic route through the Glynfrdwy (Dee) valley. The castle was the sixth-century stronghold for Eliseg, Prince of Powis, but was abandoned after only twenty years in 1282 and rapidly became a ruin; parts of a wall and the D-shaped towers remain. *(Valentine's Series, posted 1912)*

Lady Eleanor Butler and Miss Sarah Ponsonby, the Ladies of Llangollen, entertained the rich and the famous of Regency society. The ladies eloped together from Ireland and set up their home in Llangollen. *(Valentine's)*

From 1780 to 1829, Plas Newydd was home to the Ladies and it retains the Gothic appearance which they introduced. The formal gardens at the front were planted after their time. *(Unidentified, posted 1906)*

The ornate and intricately carved porch at the main entrance. The ladies spent a great deal of time converting the house to its Gothic appearance. (*Valentine's*)

The Gothic library complete with a collection of objects that once belonged to the couple. The Ladies' visitors included the rich and famous such as the Duke of Wellington, Sir Walter Scott and William Wordsworth, who unfortunately incurred some displeasure from the Ladies when he wrote a poem in which he described Plas Newydd as a 'low-roofed cott'. (*Unidentified, posted 1904*)

The gardens surrounding the house are a pleasant and tranquil retreat and a perfect setting for the house. The circles of stones (Gorsedd Stones) in the grounds of Plas Newydd were erected for the 1908 Llangollen National Eisteddfod. *(Valentine's Series)*

Three of Llangollen's celebrated inhabitants are honoured here in the parish church; firstly the seventh-century St Collen, after whom the town Llangollen takes his name and to whom the church is dedicated. Secondly, a memorial near the entrance porch commemorates the Ladies of Llangollen and both are buried in the church cemetery. *(Peacock Brand, posted 1907)*

Here we see the view downriver towards the three-arched Dee Bridge near Trevor and the Pontcysyllte aqueduct, which towers above it – a scene that has changed little in over two hundred years. The old bridge takes the Gate Road (B5434) across the river, and parts of the bridge date to 1697, although it was largely rebuilt in the eighteenth century. *(Unidentified)*

The magnificent Pontcysyllte Aqueduct (seen here from the south-west) was built to carry the Llangollen Canal (a branch of the Ellesmere Canal) across the Dyfrdwy (Dee). Opened in 1805, it took ten years to complete. The principle canal engineer was William Jessop, assisted by Thomas Telford; their magnificent structure supports an iron trough 11ft wide and 5ft 3in deep 126ft above the river on nineteen masonry piers over a length of 1,007ft. The trough was innovative and used bolted-together cast-iron plates supported underneath by cast-iron ribs. The edge of the trough – on the Llangollen side – is a few inches above the water level, and the boaters have nothing between them and a sheer drop, while a railing protects the walkers along the towpath on the opposite side. The plates were cast at the nearby Plas Kynaston Ironworks at Trevor. Equally impressive was the embankment on the south side of the aqueduct, built from spoil from the Chirk canal cutting and tunnel nearby. On the right in this view are the hillsides of the Vale of Llangollen and Panorama Walk. *(Valentine Series)*

The former ferry crossing of the Afon Dyfrdwy (Dee) at Erbistock village was probably a crossing point since the Middle Ages. The ferry was at the end of the lane beside Erbistock church and crossed between Lan-y-cefn and St Martin Way. The crossing was part of the route to Overton and operated up until 1939. *(Unidentified)*

The Grade II listed Boat Inn dates largely from the seventeenth century, and is two combined cottages. On the right is the ferry winch mechanism used to adjust the ferry cables. *(Hughes's Series, Wrexham)*

Another view of Erbistock from a little further downriver, with the ferry boat moored at the ferry steps. The two postcards on this page are also the locations of two of the villages' pubs: the famous seventeenth-century Boat Inn which takes its name from the chain ferry seen here, and the Cross Foxes at Overton Bridge, which dates to 1748 (on the left in the postcard below). *(Posted 17 March 1918, Valentine's Series)*

Overton Bridge is a little under a mile due north of Erbistock, but the distance that the river travels to the bridge is 2 miles as it meanders in a large loop towards the edge of the escarpment on which the village of Overton stands. Thomas Penson (1790–1859), County Surveyor of Montgomeryshire from 1817, designed and built Overton Bridge as a replacement for an earlier bridge which had collapsed. The earlier bridge had been built by his father who was County Surveyor for Flintshire. *(Posted 2 July 1907, Valentine's Series)*

THE RIVER DEE, BANGORISYCOED   GWENFRO SERIES

The next village downriver is Bangor-is-y-Coed, which in Welsh means 'the place of the choir'. Its original full name meant 'the place of the choir below the wood', but the name of the village was Anglicised when the Wrexham & Ellesmere Railway renamed the village station Bangor-on-Dee in 1895. Overton also had '-on-Dee' added to its name. Looking north-east above the bridge, the church and spire are at the centre of the picture, partially obscured by trees. The church, dedicated to St Dunawd, who was the first abbot of the monastery at Bangor, dates from about 1300. The abbey was rebuilt in the 1720s, and underwent further restoration in the nineteenth century. *(Gwenfro Series)*

Downstream is Bangor's five-arched stone bridge, which dates from about 1660 and was designed and built by Inigo Jones. The bridge is narrow and has eight triangular shelters for pedestrians, while the parapets are carried over the arches on each side. After a number of repairs over the centuries owing to increasingly heavy traffic and frequent flood damage, the bridge was converted to a single carriageway and weight restrictions were applied. By 1978, a new road and a new crossing of the river bypassed the bridge. *(E. Lloyd, Ruabon)*

A view of Bangor-on-Dee's High Street during one of its frequent floods, some time before July 1904. The building on the right is the Stable Yard and on the left is the Post Office and Middle Shop, while immediately to the left are locals lined up on the doorstep of the Buck Hotel. *(Unidentified, posted 1904)*

Here is a coracle fisherman on the Afon Dyfrdwy (Dee) at Craig just north of Bangor-on-Dee. In the distance is the girder bridge of the former GWR Ellesmere to Wrexham Railway. Having meandered around Bangor-is-y-Coed, the Afon Dyfrdwy (Dee) flows in a northerly direction – forming the border between England and Wales in the process – and continues to meander its way through the Cheshire plain towards Chester, adopting its English name the 'Dee' on the way. *(Unidentified)*

3

Chester

'Upon the walls it is possible to make the whole compass of the city, there being a good narrow walk upon them. The northern wall abuts upon a frightful ravine, at the bottom of which is a canal. From the western one there is a noble view of the Welsh hills.'

(*Wild Wales*, George Borrow, 1857)

The walls of Chester follow the medieval defences that enclose the city centre. It is possible to walk their entire length and view the oldest part of the city from the ramparts.

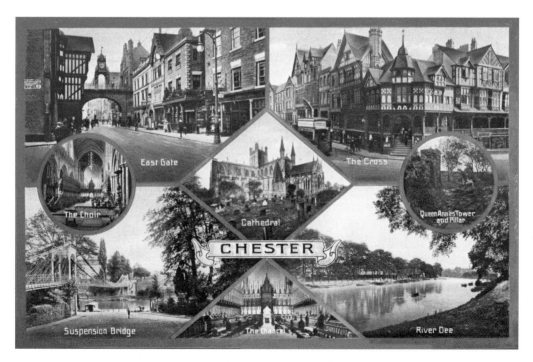

East Gate

The Cross

The Choir

Cathedral

Queen Anne's Tower and Pillar

Suspension Bridge

CHESTER

The Chancel

River Dee

(D. Clark Post Office, Chester)

River Dee, Holt Bridge.

Above Holt, the river flows through Wales or forms the border between England and Wales, while below Farndon the river lies in England until it leaves Chester. The red sandstone road bridge between Holt and Farndon spans the River Dee and crosses the boundary between Wales and England. It is a centuries-old strategic crossing point between the two countries, substantially altered during the fifteenth and sixteenth centuries, and was fought over by Parliamentary and Royalist forces during the Civil War. The eight arched pillars have pointed cutwaters and an arch exists in the causeway on the Welsh side, which was the site of a former chapel. *(The Wrench Series, posted 1905)*

THE IRON BRIDGE NEAR CHESTER.

"The Unique Series".

The Grade I listed Cast Iron Bridge crosses the Dee half a mile north of the village of Aldford and is part of the Buerton Approach to Eaton Hall. It was constructed in 1824 by William Hazledine for the 1st Marquis of Westminster. The bridge has sandstone abutments and a single arch with lattice bracing and iron railings. Aldford Lodge next to the bridge was designed and built by John Douglas in 1894 and is a Grade II listed building. The village of Aldford is probably named after the twelfth-century Robert de Aldford and there are remains of a Norman motte and bailey castle north of St John's Church which date back to the same period. The crossing was, however, even earlier and was probably a fording point for the Roman road Watling Street that passed through the centre of the village in roughly a north–south direction. *(Unidentified, posted 1905)*

The Marches Way long-distance footpath crosses the Iron Bridge and the River Dee here.

A similarly important ferry crossing point was at Eccleston, just under 2 miles further downriver from the Iron Bridge. The village is a quarter of a mile north of the ferry and was similarly divided by the Roman road Watling Street running north–south through the village. Parallel with the road is the Chester Approach to Eaton Hall. At the beginning of the twentieth century the Eccleston Ferry was a popular destination for the Chester-based river steamers. Today the ferry is no longer in service, but the ChesterBoat visits the picturesque riverside location on selected days and weekends during the summer. *(Frith's Series, F. Frith & Co., Reigate, posted 1905)*

Another view of the Eccleston Ferry and a busy day on the river. The ferry has foot passengers and a cyclist waiting to cross, but the ferryman does not seem to be there. *(Photogravure, The Milton)*

The Eaton Estate has belonged to the Grosvenor family since the early fifteenth century, and the building seen here was the Victorian Gothic Eaton Hall designed for the 1st Duke of Westminster which was completed in 1881. The house was located in 50 acres of formal gardens and a further 1,000 acres of parkland on a gentle quarter-of-a-mile eastern slope to the River Dee. The architect, Alfred Waterhouse, was adept at designing on a massive scale, having built the Natural History Museum in Kensington and Manchester Town Hall. With over 150 bedrooms, a chapel and a 180ft bell-tower, the scale of the building was in keeping with the largest public works of the time. During the Second World War, the building was used as a hospital and the Royal Naval College, after which it was leased to the Army. By the 1950s, the contents were removed and the building was finally demolished in the early 1960s, with the exception of the chapel and stable block. A new building was erected on part of the site in 1967 and modified during the 1990s, which is now home to the 6th Duke of Westminster and his family. *(Hugo Lang & Co., Liverpool)*

On the River Dee, Chester.

jws 2525

A pleasant summer's day messing about on the river with a splendid view over Queens Park and the Earls Eye from the Sandy Lane side of the Dee, *(Unidentified)*

The printed caption on the reverse side of the card says 'River Dee, above Chester. Our view is taken about half a mile above the Suspension Bridge, and shows St Paul's Church, Boughton, near which the monument to George Marsh, the Martyr stands.' Viewed from Earls Eye at Queens Park, the steamer is heading upriver to Eccleston, while on the promontory above stands St Paul's Church, designed by John Douglas and built in 1876, the spire was added in 1905. *(Valentine's Series, posted 1911)*

The view from Queens Park and the Meadows side of the river. On the opposite bank of the river is the boathouse at the end of the Parade, the probable location of the Saxon port of Chester. *(The Cestrian Series, Huke's Library, Chester)*

Enoch Gerrard, the proprietor of Queens Park, promoted the Queens Park Suspension Bridge which was built in 1852. The bridge seen here was used as a pedestrian footway across the river to join the city to the new affluent suburb of Queens Park. *(Hugo Lang & Co., Liverpool, posted 1905)*

In the 1920s, Chester Corporation took over the responsibility for Queens Park Bridge and decided to demolish it when it became unsafe. Charles Greenwood, City Engineer and Surveyor, designed and built the new bridge, seen here, which opened in 1923. The steps referred to in the postcard caption lead to St John's Church and Grosvenor Park. *(Photochrom Co. Ltd, London & Tunbridge Wells)*

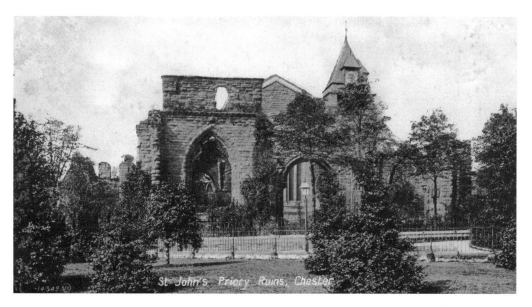

The Church of St John the Baptist was founded by King Ethelred of Mercia. Under the rule of the Normans it became the seat of Bishop Peter of Mercia who started to build the present church. Robert de Lumesay, the next bishop, moved his seat to Coventry and St John's became a Collegiate church and was partially demolished during the Dissolution of the Monasteries. The ruins of the fourteenth-century chancel, transepts and altar stand at the east end in front of the church. After the collapse of the West Tower in 1881, John Douglas (architect to the Grosvenor family) restored the porch in 1882. *(Aurochrome, Valentine's)*

In the nave are the pillars of four round arches, the substantial remains of the 1075 cathedral. The other medieval features are 20ft of the base of the twelfth-century West Tower which was never fully restored after the collapse. In 1887, John Douglas built the north-east bell tower and restored the north side of the church. *(Frith's Series, F. Frith & Co. Ltd, Reigate)*

Here we see two views from opposite sides of the river at Chester: the first shows a steamer making its way upriver about to pass under the earlier Queens Park Chain Bridge. The riverside area below is known as The Groves and is Chester's popular riverside promenade. The side where the boy stands with his fishing rod is Queens Park. *(Boots Cash Chemists, posted 1927)*

The view from the Groves bank of the Dee, directly opposite the point where the photograph above was taken. The steamer in both views is at practically the same spot on the river. The Groves were laid out by Charles Croughton in 1725 and became a fashionable riverside promenade. Alderman Charles Brown extended the promenade in 1881 to include the western end, nearest to the Old Dee Bridge. *(Boots Cash Chemists)*

8344. THE GROVES AND RIVER DEE, CHESTER.

Just upriver of the suspension bridge at the end of the promenade is the location of the Grosvenor Boat Club, the Blue Moon riverside café and the Boat House Inn. Beyond them is Grosvenor Park. *(Unidentified, posted 1926)*

RIVER DEE, CHESTER.

The nineteenth-century bandstand stands on the left amid the trees, and the new Queen's Park Suspension Bridge is in the distance. From here, riverboats departed upriver bound for the popular destinations of Eccleston Ferry and Eaton Hall. There are refreshment kiosks, a pub and landing stages for pleasure boats and rowing boats. The scene is not greatly different today: the ChesterBoat operates its service from the same spot and rowboats, pedalboats and motor boats are on hire nearby. *(Silveresque, Valentine & Sons Ltd, Dundee & London, posted 1948)*

BISHOP'S PALACE AND DEE STEAMBOAT FERRY, CHESTER.

Dee steamboats moored at The Groves with St John's Church and the Bishop's Palace rising above the trees. Today the ChesterBoat half-hour city cruise and the extended two-hour Iron Bridge cruise boats depart from the same stage, continuing a Victorian and Edwardian tradition. *(Unidentified)*

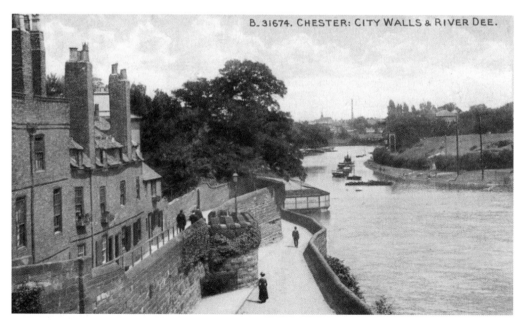

In this view of the Dee from Bridgegate, the floating swimming baths moored in the river can be seen at the side of the promenade. There was a deep end, a shallow end and changing rooms, and a canvas awning covered the whole structure. River water flowed through the baths, which were open daily during the summer months with separate sessions for women. The baths closed completely shortly after the opening of John Douglas' indoor baths in Union Street in 1901. *(Celesque, Photochrom Co. Ltd, London & Tunbridge Wells)*

The medieval Old Dee Bridge was built in about 1387, but stands on the site of numerous earlier wooden bridges and a much earlier Roman bridge which was the sole crossing from Chester into Wales. The bridge was repaired after the Civil War and widened in 1826; despite this it is still too narrow, and traffic lights control traffic. The weir was constructed in 1093 on behalf of Hugh Lupus, 1st Earl of Chester. Apart from improving navigation upriver,

it also gave a deep, fast-flowing watercourse for driving watermills. For centuries, the watercourse above the weir directed a flow of water through the two smaller arches on the right of the picture. The head of water was harnessed to power corn, fulling, snuff and flint mills, and in 1911, a hydroelectric turbine – the generator building of which is still visible today and is now used as a water pumping station. *(Unidentified)*

The Dee Corn Mill in this postcard view once stood on the north-west side of the Old Dee Bridge on the opposite side of the two smaller arches seen in the previous postcard. Hugh Lupus also used the pool for fishing, gave the Abbot of St Werburgh's Abbey tithes for a mill and fishing rights, and granted fisheries above the weir to his relatives. In the picture, the salmon fishermen have drawn their nets to catch fish trying to make their way upriver from the seaward side of the bridge. The pool, called Earl's Pool after the 1st Earl of Chester and then King's Pool after fishing rights reverted to the Crown, was the perfect location to catch fish waiting for the tide to raise them to the height of the weir. By the start of the seventeenth century, there were some eleven waterwheels grinding corn, fulling cloth and raising water, and the weir itself was causing problems with navigation along the full length of the river. The city authorities ordered that the weir and mills should be demolished, so that the water could flow rapidly and clear the accumulated silt from the Dee's navigable channels, but the mill owners resisted this move. The reduction of tidal limit and the scour of the river had taken its toll and the Dee began to silt around Chester. The city council had cut a new channel for the river in 1737 and all the mills had gone by the start of the twentieth century, some having burnt down, leaving a popular folk ballad to celebrate the Miller of Dee, 'I care for nobody, no not I, for nobody cares for me'. *(Unidentified)*

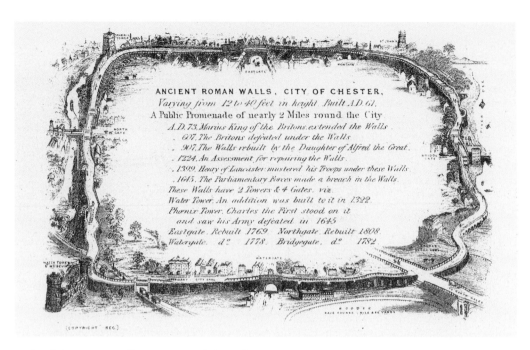

ANCIENT ROMAN WALLS, CITY OF CHESTER,
Varying from 12 to 40 feet in height. Built A.D. 61.
A Public Promenade of nearly 2 Miles round the City
A.D. 73. Marius King of the Britons extended the Walls.
. 607. The Britons defeated under the Walls
. 907. The Walls rebuilt by the Daughter of Alfred the Great.
. 1224. An Assessment for repairing the Walls.
. 1399. Henry of Lancaster mustered his Troops under these Walls.
. 1645. The Parliamentary Forces made a breach in the Walls.
These Walls have 2 Towers & 4 Gates. viz.
Water Tower. An addition was built to it in 1322.
Phœnix Tower. Charles the First stood on it
and saw his Army defeated in 1645
Eastgate. Rebuilt 1769. Northgate. Rebuilt 1808.
Watergate. d.º 1778. Bridgegate. d.º 1782.

Little of the Roman walls remains, and the walls that surround the town centre are largely medieval. Substantially complete, they offer the opportunity to walk around the entire medieval outskirts of the city. *(Unidentified)*

Here we see the city walls viewed from the Old Dee Bridge. Compare the view to the two postcards on page 58. The floating bath has been cut up and scrapped, but below the Bishop's Palace the landing stage still has its canvas coverings. In the summer months, local artists display their work along the base of the wall at the foot of the recorder steps, which descend from the city walls down to the promenade. *(Boots Cash Chemists)*

To the north of the Old Dee Bridge is the ancient Welshgate entrance through Chester's walls. Now called Bridgegate, the new gate was designed and built by Joseph Turner in 1782 and replaced the medieval entrance, which comprised of an arched gateway flanked by towers. The gates of Chester were controlled by privileged families who were able to charge taxes on goods brought into the town in payment for maintaining the gates as city defences (with the exception of the Northgate, which was the responsibility of the town's citizens). Bridgegate was in the charge of the Earl of Shrewsbury, who on occasion resided in the Bear and Billet Inn next to the gate. *(Unidentified, A real Bromide photograph)*

From 1307, Chester charged a toll for the upkeep of its walls and other defences known as murage. It was levied on all goods entering the city, at tollhouses at each gate. The practise ended in 1835 when the upkeep of the walls became the responsibility of the city council. This scene shows  a row of cottages nestled alongside the inner south-east wall with the promenade and River Dee below. Around the corner are the recorder steps, which lead down to the promenade. *(The Unique Series)*

THE EASTGATE, LOOKING TOWARDS
FOREGATE STREET, CHESTER.

A Chester city blue plaque on the archway in the street bears the following inscription:
'The Eastgate this was the site of the eastern gateway of the Roman fortress, part of which
was incorporated into the medieval gate. The present arch was built in 1768–9 at the
expense of Richard, Earl Grosvenor. The clock above commemorates the Diamond Jubilee
of Queen Victoria in 1897.' *(Unidentified)*

King Charles' Tower,
Chester
The Woodbury Series, No. 1.67.

The Phoenix Tower or King Charles I Tower is a medieval structure standing on the site of the original Roman north-east tower. In the sixteenth century, Chester had up to seventeen towers, though only a few survive to this day – perhaps the best known of which is the Phoenix Tower. The tower was used as a meeting place of city guilds, which included the Companies of Barber Surgeons, Tallow Chandlers, Painters, Glaziers, Embroiderers, Stationers, Coopers, Butchers, Weavers, Joiners and Cloth-workers. The badge of the Painters' Guild was the phoenix, and a carving of the heraldic symbol was placed over the doorway at the top of the entrance steps. *(The Woodbury Series)*

Chester, King Charles' Tower from Canal

The Phoenix Tower, seen here from the canal, was also known as the Newton Tower after the suburb it overlooked from this point. It was also known as the King Charles Tower in commemoration of the events of September 1645 during the Civil War when King Charles I, together with Chester's mayor, Sir Francis Gamul, stood on the roof and witnessed the retreat of Royalist forces after the Battle of Rowton Moor. The king escaped with a contingent of heavily armed men, while the siege of Chester continued until January 1646 – eventually brought to an end by starvation and disease. The king himself was executed on 30 January 1649 before the Palace of Whitehall. The Phoenix Tower stands high above the Chester Canal (part of the Ellesmere Canal Company) as it turns to pass through a spectacular cutting alongside the north wall on its way to Earl's Port and the River Dee. (*Frith's Series, F. Frith & Co. Ltd, Reigate*)

Pemberton's Parlour, Chester

Originally called the Goblin Tower, it was renamed Pemberton's Tower after the name of the 1840s ropemaker who watched his workers in the ropewalk, which ran alongside the walls and the row of trees. The tower was used as a fortification in the siege of Chester during the Civil War. *(N.N. Dutton, Bridge Street Row, Chester)*

The angular sandstone Bonewaldesthorne's (sometimes Bonewaldisthorne's) Tower stands on the north-west corner of the city walls, and is named after an officer of Ethelflaed's (Lady of the Mercians and daughter of Alfred the Great) forces who expelled Danish invaders from Chester. *(Valentine's Series)*

The spur wall from the Water Tower and steps back to Bonewaldesthorne's Tower and the city wall. Mounted on the roof of the tower is a camera obscura and towards the top of the spur wall is a niche and the statue of Queen Anne, rescued from the Old Exchange after it was destroyed by fire in 1862. The niche still exists but the statue mysteriously disappeared in the 1960s. *(Boots Cash Chemists, posted 1907)*

Water Tower. *Chester.*

The Water Tower (sometimes called the New Tower), built by mason John de Helpston between 1322 and 1325, is located on the north-west corner of the city walls on the end of a short spur wall, which joins on to Bonewaldesthorne's Tower. It originally stood in the estuary of the River Dee at the edge of the moorings and was used to regulate shipping and collect murage taxes into the port. The structure is high and dry now after the estuary silted, and the course of the river was diverted via the Chester 'New Cut', though it forms the impressive centrepiece to the Water Tower Gardens. *(The Wrench Series)*

By the year 400, the Roman XX Legion had abandoned the fortress of Deva Victrix, ending their occupation since AD 70. The fortress practically disappeared in the centuries that followed, and after successive incursions by Vikings and Saxons, the Normans reached Chester in 1070 and established it as a trading port. The Roman legacy remains in the plan of the city with the principle streets of the town following the former Roman street plan. Bridge Street directly overlies the Via Praetoria, Eastgate Street and part of Watergate Street the Via Principalis and Northgate Street lies over the Via Decumana. Other Roman remains include the amphitheatre, portions of wall, the base of a tower, parts of a quay and the Roman Gardens where there are a selection of columns and the hypocausts from a Roman bath, seen here. *(The Wyndham Series)*

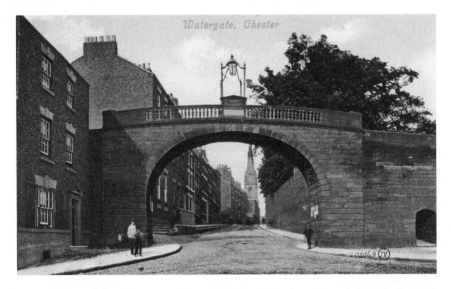

Watergate straddles Watergate Street and lies at the junction of City Walls Road, Nuns Road and New Crane Street. It is an eighteenth-century arch built to replace a medieval gateway. The old gateway was purchased from the Earl of Derby by the corporation in 1788, and was immediately demolished when it proved unsafe. Joseph Turner, who was also responsible for the design of Bridgegate, designed the present arch. *(Valentine's Series)*

Chester Corporation Tramways' electric traction system was just two years old when this card was posted in 1905. The electric tram replaced an earlier horse-drawn system and the car seen here is operating a service via Eastgate Street from the General station just over half a mile away. The station was jointly used by the GWR and the L&NWR. *(Frith's Series, F. Frith & Co. Ltd, Reigate, posted 1905)*

The Rows or Galleries are a feature of the buildings that occupy the four principle streets mentioned earlier, and run parallel with each other from the Cross, but do not extend over the whole length of each street. The origin of them is not known; the best two theories suggest that they were built on a Roman plan of buildings, or that they were defendable terraces that could be barricaded when marauding Welsh raiders entered the city. Whatever the reason, they were certainly in existence in the fourteenth century. *(Valentine's Series)*

A view of Bridge Street looking north towards the Cross along Upper Bridge Street. St Peter's Church is at the far end and is believed to stand on the site of a Roman temple. The ornate stone cross (which gave the Cross its name) was carved with figures of saints, apostles and the Virgin Mary and was destroyed in 1646 after the surrender of Chester's royalist defenders. The base of the stone cross is at Plas Newydd in Llangollen, while the remainder was hidden under the steps of St Peter's Church and some pieces ended up in the Grosvenor Museum. The city council re-erected the cross in the Roman Gardens in 1949, and replaced it in its original location when the adjoining streets were pedestrianised in 1975. *(Valentine's Series)*

At the entrance steps to the Town Hall is a blue plaque with the inscription 'Town Hall: Chester Town Hall was opened in 1869 by the Prince of Wales later Edward VII. The architect was W.H. Lynn of Belfast, whose design was chosen in a competition. It replaced the Exchange building of 1698 which stood in the centre of Northgate Street and burnt down in 1862.' (*Valentine's, posted 1935*)

Town Hall, Chester. (Floodlit)   G3864.

Opposite, bottom: At one time the Market Square held twice-weekly markets and fairs during the year. Today the row of trees have been replanted in the centre of the square and the streets are traffic-free. The buildings on the left have been replaced with an uninteresting multi-storey modern shop, but the buildings on the right remain relatively intact. The photographer who took this picture sometime before 1908 would now be standing under the entrance canopy to the Forum Shopping Centre. (*Unidentified, posted 1908*)

Old Stanley Palace,
Chester.
The Hiding Place.

Stanley Palace, built in 1591, is a Grade II listed building which stands near the site of the medieval Dominican friary in Nicholas Street. The first owner was Sir Peter Warburton, who passed the house on to his daughter Elizabeth as a dowry to the Stanleys of Alderley. After the death of her husband, Elizabeth married Sir Richard Grosvenor, and she died in 1627. By the early nineteenth century, the house was divided into three cottages and the grounds were sold for development. In 1889, Edward Henry Stanley, the 15th Earl of Derby, bought the property and it became known for a while as Derby House. In 1911, the house was a museum and curiosity shop run by E. Booth Jones. Chester City Council leases the property, which is open to the public and is administered by The Friends of Stanley Palace. *(Salmon Series)*

4265 STANLEY PALACE CHESTER

Stanley Palace is reputed to be the most haunted building in Chester and paranormal investigators frequently visit its rooms. On many occasions footsteps and muffled murmurings have been heard from the gallery, the apparition of Lady Elizabeth has been seen to walk through walls, and the ghost of the 7th Earl of Derby's manservant who allegedly betrayed him to the Royalists is seen entering the Queen Anne Room. There have also been manifestations of an old man with a walking stick and a woman playing a piano. *(Unidentified, posted 1935)*

Another of Chester's famous old buildings stands in Watergate Street. Built in 1652 it has 'God's providence is mine inheritance' written over the second-storey gable. The building was restored in 1862 and the lower shop is now Caffé Latino coffee shop, while Harriet & Dee gift shop occupies the upper Row. *(Photochrom Co. Ltd, London)*

The GWR horse-drawn flat wagon is delivering goods along Eastgate Street at the junction with St John Street and Foregate Street. A single tram rail ran under the centre of Eastgate Arch to ensure that double-decker trams had enough clearance; the system was otherwise double-tracked. *(Frith's Series, N. Dutton, Bridge Street Row, Chester)*

The view from Eastgate towards the Cross, early 1930s. The horse and cart is emerging from St Werburgh Street and the corporation bus has stopped opposite the Grosvenor Hotel by the entrance to today's Grosvenor Shopping Centre. The tram system had by this time been abandoned, although the passing loop in front of the arch is still in situ. *(Salmon Series)*

GROSVENOR
HOTEL
CHESTER

Tel. 1220

Chidley Photo

The prestigious Grosvenor Hotel is a Grade II listed building that is today better known as the Chester Grosvenor and Spa five-star hotel. Its two restaurants have the enviable accolade of four AA Rosettes and a Michelin Star. The hotel was built in 1865 and is owned by the family of the Duke of Westminster. There are sixty-eight bedrooms, twelve suites, a luxury spa and a variety of meeting rooms including an executive boardroom. *(Chidley Photo)*

Opposite the Grosvenor Hotel is St Werburgh Street and the approach to the south of Chester Cathedral – a scene which has hardly changed at all since this postcard was published. The absence of vehicles in this photograph is mirrored today, owing to the fact that nearby streets have been pedestrianised. *(Unidentified)*

CHESTER

Chester Cathedral, formerly the church of the Abbey of St. Werburgh, dates from the fifteenth century. The choir is considered to be the most beautiful in England, and the reader's pulpit the finest. In the transept, which was restored as a memorial to the late Duke of Westminster, is a magnificent altar-tomb in white marble, by Pomeroy. In the restoration of the Cathedral, both the interior and exterior was beautified and enriched. The extreme length is 375 feet, and the breadth 200 feet; nave and choir 78 feet high, and tower 120 feet.

The cathedral seen from the north-east, the explanatory caption below the emblem of Chester explains the origins and describes . . . *(Unidentified)*

. . . the nave and choir referred to in the previous postcard caption. *(Frith's Series, F. Frith & Co. Ltd, Reigate)*

The Roodee derives its name from the Saxon 'rood' for cross and the Norse word for 'eye', and is literally 'The Island of the Cross'. The Roodee was once part of the Dee Estuary and an anchorage for the port of Chester; the stone cross stood on a small offshore island. As the estuary silted up, the Roodee became a pasture for grazing animals and then a racecourse. The founder of Chester Races in the early part of the sixteenth century was Henry Gee, commemorated in the running of the Henry Gee Stakes and also by 'Gee-Gees', the nickname for racehorses. The major race run at the Roodee these days is the Chester Gold Cup formerly the Grosvenor Gold Cup, which was first presented in 1740. The Chester Race Company, which oversees the running of the course, was founded in 1893. *(Lang's Series)*

In 907, Ethelflaed erected a fort on the high ground inside the south-west extension to the Roman walls, to defend against the Danes. The Normans erected a motte and bailey castle and then a stone-built castle. Enlarged and strengthened under Henry III and then Edward I, the castle was used as a frontier post for the conquest and subjugation of the Welsh. Ending up as a store for arms, a courthouse, a garrison and a prison, Sir George Gilbert Scott undertook extensive restoration of Chester Castle between 1868 and 1876. *(Frith's Series, F. Frith & Co. Ltd, Reigate)*

Chester Castle and Combermere Monument.   "Ye Deva" Series.

The equestrian statue is of Viscount Combermere, born Stapleton Cotton, the second son of Sir Robert Salisbury Cotton and baronet of Combermere Abbey, Cheshire. He served under Wellington in Portugal as commander of the cavalry, receiving a commendation after the Battle of Salamanca on 22 July 1812. His most famous action was the capture of Bhurtpore in India. *(Unidentified)*

Chester Castle & St. Mary's Church, Chester.

Dee fishermen on the seaward side of Chester Weir. In the background is Chester Castle and Thomas Harrison's County Gaol. The tower on the left is the one remaining Norman feature: a large, square tower, called Julius Agricola's Tower. St Mary's Church is on the right. *(F. Richardson, Foregate Street, Chester, posted 1914)*

The salmon fishermen lived and worked here in the early part of the twentieth century in Greenaway Street and Handbridge, and fished a number of select spots below the Old Dee Bridge. During the twentieth century, fishing declined and to counter this, 'Salmon Steps' were built in the weir, and fisheries were opened to improve stocks. The Dee is a salmon river and the principle reaches for angling are its tributaries upstream of Bangor-on-Dee, with trout and coarse fish downstream in the canalised river and estuary. A few salmon, flounder and shrimp fishermen still fish in the estuary. *(The Star Series, G.D. & D., London)*

The magnificent Grosvenor Bridge (1833) designed by Thomas Harrison which at the time was the widest single-arch in the world. The course of the River Dee curves around an S-shaped bend at this point and flows through a straight artificial channel for 5 miles into its estuary. *(Lang's Series, Hugo Lang & Co., Liverpool)*

4

The Dee Estuary in North Wales

'Resuming the journey to Chester from Rhyl, Mostyn celebrated for its collieries is passed, and the traveller arrives at Holywell station. About a mile from this, on the side of a hill, is St Winefride's Well, which gives its name to the town. The well is situated close to the church and throws up thirty tons of water per minute. It is highly spoken of for bathing purposes. Passing Bagillt, we come to Flint. To the left of the station can be seen, rising up from a rocky promontory on the shore, the ruins of Flint Castle, the scene of poor Richard II's humiliation and betrayal. No other place of interest is met with until, leaving Wales behind, and passing the Saltney Junction, we enter the cutting through Brewers Hall Hill, from which Cromwell bombarded Chester, cross the Dee, over the largest cast iron girder bridge in the Kingdom.'

(London & North Western Tourists Picturesque Guide,
London & North Western Railway Company, 1876)

Following the railway from Hawarden Bridge there are walks along the Dee towards Chester on the canalised section of river and towards the estuary at Flint Marsh, Greenfield Valley Park at Holywell, Mostyn and Ffynnongroew Woods, Point of Ayr and Talacre Sands.

HAWARDEN CASTLE

Above: This postcard shows Hawarden Castle, sometimes referred to as Hawarden House. It was built in 1752 and its most famous residents were William E. Gladstone (1809–98), former Prime Minister, 'Grand Old Man' and 'The People's William'. He lived there with his wife Catherine (née Glynne) who was born at Hawarden Castle in 1812. She was heiress to the Hawarden Estate and after she married Gladstone in 1839 the couple made Hawarden their home. Catherine had eight children and the family descendants still live at Hawarden. *(J. Beagles & Co Ltd, London, posted 1906)*

In this multiple-view card are the remains of the Norman castle slighted during the Civil War and never restored. As a ruin it become part of the gardens of Hawarden House. In the eighteenth and nineteenth centuries the village had a market, and prospered on coal, iron, and brick manufacture. *(Unidentified)*

Looking directly down over Connah's Quay with the Shotton Steelworks and Hawarden Bridge just visible at the centre right. The town of Connah's Quay developed in the nineteenth century on the banks of the canalised Dee, 6 miles downriver from Chester. By the end of the century it was a thriving Deeside port. With a shipbuilding industry and a large quay, the Irish Coal Company sailed vessels to Liverpool, Dublin and North Wales from here. *(The Wrench Series)*

The Wrexham, Mold & Connah's Quay Railway (WM&CQR) built the railway bridge over the River Dee at Hawarden in 1890. The company later became part of the Great Central Railway (GCR) and after the 1923 grouping, the London & North Eastern Railway (LNER). The bridge is on the Wrexham to Bidston line and there are two stations either side of the bridge. Beyond the bridge is Shotton Steelworks on Deeside, originally owned by John Summers & Sons. It later became part of British Steel, after which it was bought by Corus, which now operates it. The town of Shotton existed in Saxon times and is now largely continuous with Connah's Quay and Queensferry. *(Unidentified)*

Connahs Quay.   River Dee and Wharf.

The quay from the Dee Cut. The town and the quay probably get their name from Mr Connah, the former landlord of the Old Quay House public house on the docks. The parish of Connah's Quay was created in 1844. *(The Wrench Series, posted 1907)*

The Wharf, Connah's Quay.

The dock and wharfs were served by the WM&CQR and the Buckley Railway. Goods traffic mainly consisted of fire-clay and pottery products, while further downriver at Kelsterton a large brewery was built which was served by the Chester and Holyhead Railway. *(Unidentified)*

In the centre of the view is the 1920s Courtaulds Textile Castle Works, formerly the Muspratt Chemical Factory. In 1917 Courtaulds also bought the British Glanzstoff works and renamed the factory Aber Works. Flint Docks had four large wharves and coal depots serving the Pickering & Ormiston and Flint Marsh Collieries. Beyond the factories is the River Dee and the Wirral coast. The scenery around the town of Flint is still largely rural. *(Valentine's Sepiatone)*

Flint was the first castle built by Edward I during his conquest of Wales in the thirteenth century, and was a day's march from Chester. The name 'flint' is a reference to the low sandstone promontory below the castle, jutting out into the salt marsh. The castle was built to defend a ford crossing of the Dee, which was used at low tide. The castle took approximately eight years to complete using stone quarried and transported on rafts from Shotwick, and sandstone blocks from Ness on the Wirral coast. The Dee Estuary lapped around the north and east sides of the castle, while on the landward side there was a ditch with stone revetment and an outer bailey. Tidal waters from the Dee filled the 20ft-deep ditch and entry to the castle was through a square tower with a gateway and portcullis, by way of a drawbridge across the ditch. *(Unidentified, posted 1912)*

ST. WINIFREDE'S WELL, HOLYWELL. (13)   W. 127

Holywell takes its name from the town's major attraction: St Winefride's Holy Well, a shrine to a seventh-century nun. The water from the well supposedly has healing powers and the well has been a site of pilgrimage since that time, and possibly earlier. Holywell is known as the 'Lourdes of Wales' because of it. Lady Margaret Beaufort built the buildings here in the early sixteenth century to commemorate the victory of her son Henry Tudor over King Richard III at Bosworth Field. The spring flows into a chamber in the basement to St Winefride's Chapel and waters flow out to an outdoor bathing pool. The chapel has a beautiful corbelled ceiling with carvings. The chapel stands next to a church . . . *(Valentine's)*

... and there has been a church on the site since the eleventh century. The well was also known to the Romans, but was popularised when St Winefride, the niece of St Beuno, was murdered by Prince Caradoc. After she had fought off the prince's unwanted advances, she ran to her uncle for safety. Pursuing her, the enraged Prince Caradoc drew his sword and cut off her head, which rolled down a steep slope; water sprang from the spot where it came to rest. As St Beuno laid Winefride's head on her shoulders bringing her back to life, Prince Caradoc was swallowed by the ground. Next to the Chapel is St James' Church, the site of St Beuno's church. *(Woodall, Minshall Thomas Co., Wrexham & Oswestry)*

Holywell is a traditional Welsh market town with late Georgian and Victorian buildings and little has changed over the years. The main trunk road in the area, the A55, bypasses the town to the north a little further behind the point where this photograph was taken (probably from Pen-y-ball top). The town's principle industrial area, Greenfield (the area in the centre of this view), is a little over a mile away on the banks of the Dee Estuary. The industrial heritage of Greenfield is preserved in the Greenfield Heritage Park. The site also includes Basingwerk Abbey, a Cistercian house founded in 1132. *(Photochrom Co. Ltd, London & Tunbridge Wells)*

The town centre has changed little apart from being pedestrianised. The town hall on the left still has its clock, and practically all the buildings seen here have survived. Only the appearance of shop frontages and the type of goods sold are an indication of the many years that have passed since this card was posted. *(Valentine's Series, posted 1919)*

Pen-y-ball monument was erected in 1893 to commemorate the marriage of the Duke of York to Princess Mary of Teck. Pen-y-ball is at the edge of the Halkyn Mountain range and is an Urban Common and Open Access Area, in sight of the Dee Estuary, which is less than 2 miles away. The whole mountain was heavily mined, quarried and surrounded by limekilns. From the Middle Ages onwards Pen-y-ball was a site for lead smelting which was carried out in dug out holes called 'boles'. *(Schotcher's Series, Posted 1912)*

Whitford (its Welsh name Chwitffordd) is a pleasant hillside village at the head of a tree-covered dale, which stretches 2 miles to the Dee coast. The inn takes its name from the Mostyn family, prominent landowners in the district. The family owned some 4,000 acres of land and properties, which included a forty-room mansion with a private chapel and farm, 150 cottages, public houses, eighty-odd farms and small holdings, lead mines, a limestone quarry and the Point of Ayr

The Mostyn Arms, Whitford, Holywell.

Colliery at Talacre. The lands were sold after the death of the 10th Baronet Sir Pyers Charles Mostyn in 1917. In addition, another of the family's possessions was Basingwerk Abbey and in 1923, Miss Clementina Mostyn bequeathed it to the Office of Works (now CADW). The pub still exists although it changed its name to the Huntsman, possibly to avoid confusion with the similarly named Mostyn Arms Hotel in Mostyn. *(Unidentified)*

The Offa's Dyke Path is a mile south-west of the village. Offa's Dyke extends the whole length of the Marches and crosses the River Dee at the Vale of Llangollen.

Point-of-Ayr Lighthouse.

Burrows' Series
Prestatyn.

The Point of Ayr (Y Parlwr Du) lighthouse stands 100ft tall to the north of Talacre beach at the tip of North Wales, and at the very mouth of the Dee Estuary. The lighthouse was built in 1776 to guide ships in the Irish Sea and in the coastal waters of the Dee Estuary, but was superseded in 1844 by an offshore metal pile lighthouse commissioned by Trinity House, which was itself replaced in 1883 by a lightship. *(J.T. Burrows & Sons, Prestatyn, dated 1923)*

5

The Wirral's West Coast

'The beautiful country on the Wirral Peninsula "twixt Mersey and Dee" is now open out to health and pleasure seekers. Through bookings, Day, and Short Date Excursions have been introduced by the Cheshire Lines, Great Central, Lancashire & Yorkshire and other companies to HOYLAKE and WEST KIRBY, from Bradford, Huddersfield, Halifax, Leeds, Bury, Bolton, Preston, Manchester, Ashton, Stalybridge, Stockport, Warrington, Widnes, and other stations in Lancashire and Yorkshire.'

(J.H. Burns, Wirral Railway, New Brighton, *The Railway Year Book for 1913*)

The railways were certainly responsible for bringing holidaymakers and day-trippers to Hoylake and West Kirby. People came to escape the grimy towns, mills and factories of Lancashire and Yorkshire, and for the young, paddling was definitely their intention. Hoylake and West Kirby both developed into fashionable resorts at the end of the nineteenth century and the beginning of the twentieth century. Prior to the arrival of the railways, both were little more than seaside villages. The Deeside ports on the Wirral, Parkgate, Dawpool and the quay at Neston had already gone into decline because, after the canalisation of the Dee in 1737, Chester's New Cut had caused the natural flow of the river to move towards the Welsh coast and Flint, and the Wirral coast began to silt up.

The decline of shipping in the Dee and the rise of Liverpool as the significant port in the North-West made the Wirral coast and the Dee something of a backwater. However, the towns and villages along the Wirral coast of the estuary benefited by developing into popular residential areas, with their inhabitants commuting to work in Liverpool, Birkenhead and Chester via the railways. The Wirral Way follows a former railway from Neston to West Kirby and there are many hillside and coastal paths to explore.

Paddling at Hoylake.
(*Valentine's Series*)

This is how the old Ness village appeared in the early part of the twentieth century. The houses here stand on the Neston to Burton Road just before the village crossroads with Well Lane and Mill Lane. The village is now largely given over to modern housing and a little to the south is Ness Gardens. Arthur Kilpin Bulley, a Liverpool cotton broker and keen botanist, founded the gardens in 1898 and they were bequeathed to the University of Liverpool by his daughter Lois after his death in 1948. *(Frith's Series, F. Frith & Co. Ltd, Reigate)*

The Bushell Memorial Fountain at the crossroads in the centre of Neston was erected in honour of Christopher Bushell, a Liverpool wine merchant and local benefactor who lived a mile outside the town at Hinderton Hall. Bushell sank the well at Neston Cross and laid on the first fresh water supply to the town; his memorial fountain was connected to this same supply. The brick-built tower behind the fountain is Jackson's Tower and it stood over George Jackson's chemist shop. Local legend says that it once housed a chiming clock that drowned out the ring of the chimes from the parish church of St Mary and St Helen – the clock was removed after protests. The road that heads off into the distance is Parkgate Road. *(Hugo Lang & Co., Liverpool)*

Neston High Street looking towards the junction with Bridge Street. Both buildings on the right have been demolished to make room for road-widening, but the block on the left still exists. The inn is now a bank and the adjoining building further down is a greengrocers. Bridge Street leads directly down

to the Wirral Way and the bridge which takes it across the road, while half a mile further on lie the old colliery quay and the Dee Estuary. In the late eighteenth century and for the whole of the nineteenth century, the area was the site of intense industrial activity and coal mining; the last mine closed in 1927. Coal was loaded onto ships bound for Chester and the inland canals, or North Wales, the Isle of Man and Ireland. *(Valentine's Series)*

Parkgate Road, **NESTON**.

Parkgate Road heads down from Neston for about a mile to the Dee Estuary and the quayside at Parkgate. The building immediately on the right is Elmhurst House, which dates to the early part of the eighteenth century; the building beyond it is Elmgrove House, built in the late eighteenth century. *(T.S.B & C., posted 1904)*

The full length of Parkgate promenade, which extends for half a mile from Station Lane to Boathouse Lane. Mostyn House School is on the right and the Dee Estuary is on the left. The sea wall was built as a promenade and was never used as a quay; in the days of the packet boats bound for Ireland, ships would anchor in the channel and passengers would be rowed out in boats. A group of fishermen look on from the parapet of the sea wall as two donkeys and their riders pause for the photograph. *(Unidentified, posted 1906)*

Schoolmaster Edward Price moved his school from Tarvin to Parkgate and founded Mostyn School in the summer of 1855 in rented buildings. The original school buildings included the Mostyn Arms Hotel, formerly the George Inn, seen here in this 1902 postcard. The façade of the hotel was dramatically altered in 1932 when the front wall had to be strengthened. The hotel proprietor was Mrs Esther Briscoe, who refurbished the George Inn and reopened it as a hotel in 1819. When she died in 1855, the railway speculator Thomas Brassey held the mortgage and after his death in 1870, the property was bought freehold by the next headmaster, the Revd A.S. Grenfell (nephew to Mrs Price). His eldest son Algernon became headmaster in 1890. *(Maycock, Parkgate, posted 1907)*

Parkgate, from the Shore.

The shoreline at Parkgate looks a little different today. The whole front is salt marsh, which rises to over halfway up the sea wall. The building on the left is Balcony House; built in the mid-eighteenth century, it had a large assembly room at the back, used by visitors to Parkgate. The two buildings in the centre are Hilbre House (demolished in the 1960s) and on its right the Ship Inn. At the gap in front of the two buildings is Drury Lane, where in 1935 William 'King' Kingsley, a dairyman from Neston, built his famous ice cream parlour, Nicholls of Parkgate. (*J. Geo. Davis, photographer, Port Sunlight, posted 1908*)

copyright
V. CROOK.   THROUGH AN ATTIC WINDOW, PARKGATE.

The view from the attic window – actually Parkgate Coffee Shop window – shows the promenade awash during a high tide on a stormy day in the late 1930s. On the right is the so-called 'Donkey Stand' jutting out into the estuary; a building once stood here and housed Parkgate's first assembly room in 1780. It later became a sea baths, and the building was demolished during the middle of the nineteenth century, though by then the sea walls had been built around it. (*V. Crook*)

THE PROMENADE, PARKGATE.

"The Unique Series"

From the middle of the seventeenth century most of Parkgate belonged to the Mostyns. Sir Roger Mostyn petitioned for a market at Great Neston in 1728; the Royal Charter was granted and the town prospered with trade from all around Cheshire and shipping between Chester and North Wales – using the River Dee and its estuary. Increasingly, as Neston Quay began to silt up, masters anchored their vessels further downstream at Parkgate, and by the end of the eighteenth century Parkgate had become Chester's principle outlying port. The houses here now look far less austere then they did when this postcard was posted in 1906. *(Unique Series, posted 1906)*

PARADE FROM MOSTYN SQUARE, PARKGATE.

Copyright. V. CROOK.

The square, looking north. The lamppost seems to have lost its shade and gas mantle, and today the building on the right is the Marsh Cat Restaurant. After the last sailing packets moved to Liverpool in the 1820s and the fishermen moved to Heswall in the late 1930s, Parkgate and the silting estuary settled down to just receiving visitors keen to sample the pleasures of this picturesque seaside resort on the Dee. *(V. Crook)*

Until the late 1930s, the main course of the Dee ran parallel to the Wirral shoreline. The so-called 'Denna Gutter' was the deep channel that ran from the early Denhall (Denna) Colliery past the old quay at Neston, and past Parkgate. The two types of fishing vessels seen here are the single-mast Morecambe Bay Prawner, locally referred to as a 'nobby', and the conventional rowboat nicknamed a 'punt'. The buildings immediately behind the 'punt' are, to the left, Overdee and to the right of it Parkgate Convalescent Home, which was demolished in the 1950s. *(Unidentified, posted 1912)*

WAITING FOR THE LOW WATER. PARKGATE

Walking up middle slip is a fisherman with a hand shrimp net. The technique was to trawl the edge of the tide or flooded pools at low water. The building on the right is the Watch House, which was built in 1720 and was used as a customs lodge from 1800. By 1828 it was home to Mary Cunningham, Parkgate's bathhouse keeper. From the eighteenth century, sea bathing had become a popular pastime at Parkgate for medicinal as well as pleasure purposes. Emma Lyon, later Lady Hamilton and mistress to Lord Nelson, stayed at Parkgate to take salt baths for a skin ailment. *(Wm. Ledsham, Clontarf Café, Parkgate, Cheshire, posted 1931)*

The tide and wind create a heavy swell that breaks over the low sea wall beyond the middle slipway, seen here in 1939. (*V. Crook*)

At the end of the promenade is the Boat House Café, seen here shortly after it was built in 1926. An inn called the Beer House stood on the site in 1620. It was later renamed the Ferry House after a ferry landing place was established in 1814. The ferry operated between Parkgate and Flint, and the proprietor of the inn and owner and of the boat was a Mr J. Davies. When the Mostyn Estate at Parkgate was sold in 1849, the inn, which was then known as the Pengwern Arms, was sold to Thomas Johnson and the ferry service went to Joseph Railton. Johnson also operated a coach and omnibus via Neston and Willaston to Hooton railway station, which opened in 1840 and, at the time, was owned by the Birkenhead, Lancashire & Cheshire Junction Railway. The ferry service came to an abrupt end with the death of Railton in 1863, and the premature death of Johnson and his brother who drowned trying to land the ferryboat in 1864. (*Miss Katherine Smith, The Boathouse, Parkgate, Cheshire*)

THE MIDDLE SLIPWAY, PARKGATE.

A final view of Parkgate with the fishermen's punts on the middle slipway. *(V. Crook)*

Riverbank Road, as its name implies, ends on the banks of the River Dee. These buildings, which date from the late 1890s, are just a few yards away from the river. *(State Publishing Co., South Castle Street, Liverpool, posted 1907)*

A view of the village of Lower Heswall. In the Domesday Book the village was called 'Eswelle', which means 'Hazel Well', and it started as a collection of scattered cottages and small farms centred on St Peter's Church. By the mid-nineteenth century, the village began to expand when wealthy merchants from Liverpool built holiday retreats overlooking the Dee Estuary. The building of houses continued and the village grew to encompass the local townships of Gayton, Irby, Pensby and Thingwall. *(Harrop's Ltd, Liverpool, posted 1907)*

Published by Hugo Lang & Co, Liverpool. 70921

Church & Vicarage. **Heswall.** Cheshire.

Two views from the Dale, which include Heswall's parish church, St Peter's. Parts of the tower date back to the fourteenth and fifteenth centuries, but the whole church was rebuilt in 1739, and again in 1879 after fire damaged the building following a lightning strike. Here looking up from rectory close . . . *(Unidentified, posted 1903)*

Heswall, Parkgate in the Distance

. . . and here looking south-east along the Dee coast towards Parkgate. *(Unidentified)*

The slopes of the Heswall shore extended northwards from the slipway at the end of Banks Road to the end of Station Road at Thurstaston. *(H. Middleton Jones, Photographer & Publisher, Heswall, dated 1916)*

The view from Heswall Dales, an area of sandy heath with spectacular views of the Dee. The Dales has been designated a Site of Special Scientific Interest and is also a local nature reserve. *(Perfection Series)*

> *The Wirral Way runs across the bottom of this view and access can be gained via either Riverbank Road or Banks Road.*

Nets on the shore and a rising tide in the Dee Estuary at Heswall looking out over Dawpool and Holywell Banks and the distant Welsh coastline. *(F. Hale, publisher, Heswall).* The view is reminiscent of the famous poem:

> O Mary, go and call the cattle home,
> And call the cattle home,
> And call the cattle home,
> Across the sands of Dee.
> The western wind was wild and dank with foam
> And all alone went she.
> 'The Sands of Dee', Charles Kingsley (1819–75)

The Shore, Heswall

The two local fishermen are possibly Richard Evans and William 'Racko' Higgins, seated on the side of their shrimp boat at Heswall. As marshland began to extend into Gayton Sands, it became increasingly difficult to land catches at Parkgate. Inevitably, fishermen began to anchor their boats at Heswall and Thurstaston and collect their catches in hand carts and then vans driven onto the beach. The message written on the reverse side of this postcard says in typical wish-you-were-here'style, 'Dear John – We are enjoying ourselves very much and the weather is beautiful we had a picnic on this shore yesterday. There were a lot of people on the shore. I am trying to get brown.' *(Unidentified, posted August 1937)*

A delightful message on the back of this Thurstaston card says, 'tea at the Cottage Loaf fresh salmon, etc. all very nice. Then we walked up the big hill what a lovely view all the north of Wales & Hoylake, was grand we went on to West Kirby & Hoylake back to Liverpool and home for quarter past ten, after a lovely day out.' *(Frith's Series, F. Frith & Co. Ltd, Reigate)*

Thurstaston is home to the visitor centre for the Wirral Way, Britain's designated first country park, which opened in 1973. The park follows a linear route along a disused railway line from Hooton to Grange Road at West Kirby. The railway opened in stages; the first section between Hooton and Parkgate was opened in 1866 to serve the villages of Willaston and Neston. Later extended to West Kirby in 1886, Thurstaston station opened to passengers at the same time, along with a new Parkgate station, Heswall and West Kirby (Birkenhead). Kirby Park station opened in 1894 and Caldy in 1909. Originally operated as a joint line by the GWR and L&NWR, British Railways withdrew all passenger services in 1956 when the service proved to be no longer economically viable. The line closed entirely in 1962 and the rails were pulled up; the land lying derelict for many years. In 1969, Cheshire County Council purchased the old trackbed and together with the Countryside Commission established the country park and the 12-mile footpath. After 1974 and the reorganisation of local government, Cheshire County Council and Wirral Borough Council jointly took on the responsibility of looking after the park. The station at Hadlow Road in Willaston was restored to how it would have looked in British Railways times and a small section of rail was reinstated. Neston rock cuttings were cleared of accumulated debris and the overgrown trackbed alongside the Dee Estuary was cleared of undergrowth. The Wirral Way follows the banks of the estuary northwards for 6 miles from Neston through Parkgate, Heswall, Thurstaston and Caldy and there are tantalising glimpses of the river for most of the way. It is also a cycle way and separate bridle path. The wildlife is varied: squirrels, badgers and foxes, as well as many species of bird including lapwings, meadow pipits, terns and occasional birds of prey.

Thurstaston beach path. Written on the back of the card is the message, 'Hello old dears just thought I'd send you a peep at one of my favourite haunts on the Wirral. Ralf is with us and needless to say is enjoying it too, cheerio – Margaret.' *(Frith's Series, F. Frith & Co. Ltd, Reigate)*

The stairway to the unspoilt beach still exists unchanged, and is easily reached from the end of Station Road and the visitor centre car park at Thurstaston.

West Kirby is a long-established seaside resort on the north-western extremity of the Wirral peninsula, with many vantage points on surrounding high ground to look down onto the mouth of the Dee Estuary. *(Valentine's Series, posted 1911)*

One such vantage point is from Caldy Hill, a sandstone outcrop covering an area of some 250 acres. Today the hillside viewed from Caldy railway station has much more woodland than in this scene from the first decade of the twentieth century. When the hill was predominantly heathland, there were fewer trees to obscure the view of the estuary. *(Valentine's Series)*

The little village of Caldy nestles on the southern slope of Caldy Hill, and apart from free-roaming geese, is little changed today. On the left are the steps to the Church of the Resurrection and All Saints, which was originally the school house; the buildings on the right still exist. Caldy has a bus service to Chester and the bus passes along this road Mondays to Saturdays. *(Ryder's Series, West Kirby)*

The timber-framed 'Reading Room' once belonged to the school, though it is now used as the church hall. Built in 1883 it has a rock-faced basement and a jettied ground floor. The central gable window as it appears here once protruded further out into the road, but had to be modified when it became a hazard for the buses and increased road traffic. *(The British Mirror Series, posted 1911)*

WEST KIRBY FROM CALDY HILL

15493

This is the view from Caldy Hill in the 1940s, looking down onto the outskirts of West Kirby from the south and the Dee Estuary with Hilbre Island on the horizon. *(J. Salmon & Co., Sevenoaks, posted 1949)*

The Column, West Kirby

Ships entering the Dee Estuary or bound for Liverpool once used a windmill on Caldy Hill as a navigation beacon. When the mill was destroyed in a storm, the trustees of Liverpool Docks erected the 60ft tall Mariners Beacon in 1841, to aid navigation for ships miles out at sea. The beacon stands at the edge of Caldy Hill between village lane and the aptly named Column Road. *(Valentine's Series, posted 1916)*

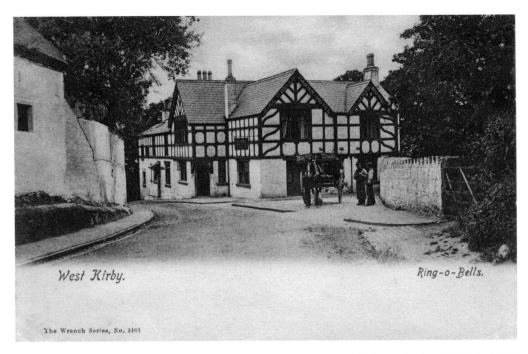

A little further down village lane is the Ring o' Bells, a picturesque public house built in 1880. Its black and white timbers and whitewashed walls remain unchanged to this day, and it continues to serve real ale along with meals. The horse-drawn dray is from Birkenhead Brewery Co. The draymen strike a relaxed pose while the photographer takes their picture. *(The Wrench Series)*

Another one of West Kirby's vantage points to view the Dee is Grange Hill, with commanding views of Hoylake, West Kirby the Dee Estuary and the Wirral coast. *(Valentine's Series)*

General View from Grange Hill   West Kirby

From this vantage point, looking south-west over the Dee Estuary is the Welsh coast, approximately in line with Holywell. In the centre of the view is the tower of St Bridget's Church at West Kirby, with the GWR and L&NWR joint line from Hooton just behind it. To the right is a puff of smoke from a steam locomotive approaching West Kirby. *(The Wrench Series, posted 1904)*

This time looking in a westerly direction from the same vantage point, once again the view is of the Dee Estuary and the distant coastline of Wales in the direction of Point of Ayr. Banks Road post office, where this card was purchased, is among the buildings in the left-hand corner. *(J.H. Lawton, Banks Road Post Office, West Kirby)*

This delightful postcard, photographed at Liscard & Poulton station on the Wirral Railway's West Kirby & Seacombe branch, was sold nationally with a number of captions each beginning with 'Arrived Safely at . . .' and then the name of the town or city. The actual station where the photograph was taken no longer exists (it is now under the M53), but the line saw countless trains full of holidaymakers and commuters making their way to and from Liverpool, Hoylake and West Kirby via the Seacombe ferry crossing of the River Mersey. *(Publisher unidentified)*

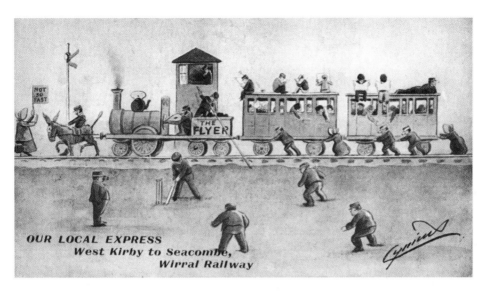

Another light-hearted postcard depicting the services offered by the Wirral Railway. The message written on the back of the card says, 'thought you might like to see the swiftness of the Wirral Railway, Love to all Martha.' (*Dynicus Publishing Co. Ltd, Tayport, Fife, posted 1909*)

A more conventional railway theme is depicted in this postcard view of West Kirby station with its clock tower (built in 1896) as seen from Grange Road. The building replaced an earlier station, which opened with the line in 1878. The station building looks very much the same today, and the buildings in the centre of the view remain, although the Dee Hotel a little further beyond was rebuilt with a mock Tudor façade. The large building on the right is the Christian Institute which dates from 1892; it stood on the corner of the Crescent and was demolished in 1963, having been replaced by an office block. (*Langs Series, posted 1904*)

The Crescent is home to West Kirby's most smart and stylish shops seen from the equally chic Banks Road. The town developed into a fashionable seaside resort after the arrival of the railways and the growth of the Victorian pastime of sea bathing for health, which was a natural progression from an earlier obsession with inland spas. *(The Wrench Series, posted 1908)*

The Victorian idea of healthy and invigorating seaside air, and a location away from the polluted cities prompted the founders of the Children's Convalescent Home to build their hospital in Moels Road in 1899. The hospital benefited thousands of children suffering from endemic diseases such as tuberculosis, rheumatic fever and rickets, before better healthcare and antibiotics reduced their plight. The building is now home to the non-maintained West Kirby Residential School, a day and residential special needs school for children. *(Caxton Series)*

Ashton Park was another of West Kirby's amenities. Laid out between 1896 and 1899, it was named after its owner Miss Elizabeth Ashton, and purchased by the council after her death in 1935. The park, cut in two by the Wirral Way, follows the former GWR and L&NWR joint Hooton to West Kirby railway. The church tower visible is St Bridget's and Church Road railway bridge is on the right of the picture. *(Valentine's Series, posted 1911)*

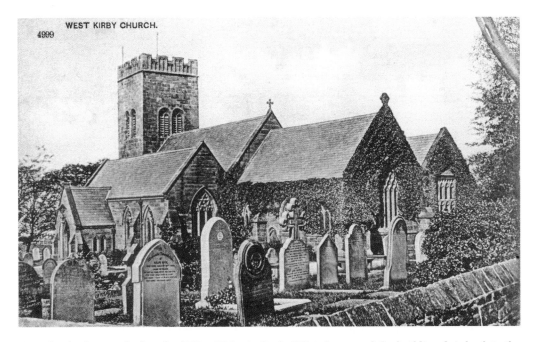

St Bridget's, the parish church of West Kirby, is Grade II listed; parts of the building date back to the fourteenth century but the building was largely reconstructed in 1869/70. The church was the centre of the old village of West Kirby, which comprised a number of small cottages, shops, the Ring o' Bells pub and farms in a predominantly agricultural community. *(Publisher unidentified, posted 1905)*

The Tower, West Kirby.

The Dee's beaches at West Kirby attracted young and old alike, many visiting for the day, others staying for longer in boarding houses. *(Cable Series, Harrop's Ltd, Liverpool)*

Tells Tower.   West Kirby.

Tell's Tower is now part of a private residence, seen here from the edge of the Marine Lake and Sandy Lane, which is home to West Kirby Sailing Club. The tower stands at the corner of the garden wall of the former Hilbre House, and was built in 1871 to commemorate a dog. The dog called Tell perished while saving his master, the Revd John Cummings McDonald, from drowning. The Revd McDonald later erected the monument in the garden of his home. *(The Wrench Series, posted 1908)*

Victoria Gardens (referred to here as the Marine Gardens) are at the corner of South Parade, overlooked by the Victorian Terrace in Victoria Drive. West Kirby grew rapidly after the arrival of the railways; streets radiated in all directions from the station in Grange Road. Rows of houses were built on a grid pattern of streets from Banks Road and the South Parade, and the planners of the new resort town were ever-conscious of the need for leisure amenities. *(Valentine's Series, posted 1922)*

By the 1890s, West Kirby was an established resort and the promenade built in 1899 was definitely the place to be seen. The couple taking a stroll are heading north towards the wooden boathouse at the edge of the Marine Lake opposite Dee Lane. *(H. Turner, The Crescent, West Kirby, posted 1917)*

Promenade, West Kirby

Another view of the promenade, this time looking in the opposite direction towards Sandy Lane and Tell's Tower. *(Valentine's Series, posted 1920)*

'A few minutes' train journey from Hoylake brings the traveller to WEST KIRBY, "Here", says the *Illustrated London News*, "one finds all the elements of the picturesque. So soft yet invigorating is the air that it deserves the title of a second Mentone".'

(J.H. Burns, Wirral Railway, New Brighton, *The Railway Year Book for 1913*)

Marine Lake and Boat-House, West Kirby

The chairman and officials of Hoylake and District Council officially opened the Marine Lake and the parade in October 1899. The wooden boathouse (built in 1903) was on the northern edge of the 52-acre, 5ft deep lake. The building has since been replaced, and a new building is home to the Wirral Sailing Centre. *(Valentine's Series, posted 1906)*

The public open-air baths were located at the southern end of the marine lake. The advertisement on the postcard dated 1927 says, 'with best wishes from Hoylake & West Kirby, the ideal family resorts, publicity Bureau.' *(Unidentified, posted 1927)*

The impressive looking Hydropathic Hotel was reopened in 1896 after extensive rebuilding of the earlier 1890 hotel. A smart and stylish building, it proclaimed itself the 'Sanatorium of the North' and took advantage of the facilities offered by the Marine Lake. In 1901, a group of gentlemen formed the West Kirby Sailing Club at the hotel to sail dinghies on the Marine Lake. The club has now relocated to premises in Sandy Lane, and its members continue to sail the lake and Dee Estuary. The Hoylake District Council also hired boats out by the hour to promote the more sedate pastime of rowing around the lake. The hotel was demolished in the late 1960s and was replaced by housing, after the fashion for sea bathing and holidaying at the British seaside declined. *(Atherton's Series, posted 1905)*

A sign of the future in a time when the motorcar and motorbike were still a rare sight. The scene today is greatly different – the baths and Hydro Hotel have gone, and many more parked cars now occupy the promenade. *(Celesque, Photochrom Co. Ltd, London & Tunbridge Wells)*

The message on the card says, 'having a nice quiet time here,' which is hard to believe if the scene here is anything to go by. The holidaymakers and day-trippers in this photograph are looking on and listening to the band playing on the shore, while children dig in the sand and take donkey rides. *(Valentine's Series, posted 1914)*

The message on this card posted on 25 September 1907 says, 'Dear little Arthur, I am sure you would like to be here watching the donkeys and digging in the sand. There are such a lot of little boys and girls and beautiful dogs, which delight in swimming for sticks in the water.' *(Valentine's Series, posted 1907)*

The Dee was not always so tranquil, and gales blowing from the Irish Sea could make the estuary inhospitable. Contrast the scene here with the two previous cards, the storm and the high water covers the same beach where the band played, and the donkeys gave rides while children dug in the sand. *(Wilson Series, The Crescent)*

Another contrast: rough seas at Tell's Tower. Compare this to the two cards on page 116 which show the same spot when the tide is out on a pleasant sunny day. *(Valentine's Series, posted 1914)*

The name of Hoylake comes from 'High Lake' and 'Heye-pol', which was once a tidal pool, in places 20ft deep. The pool extended several miles between Meols and Hilbre and was protected by a sandbank known as Hoyle Bank. It provided a safe anchorage for ships, which were too large to sail up the Dee Estuary to the port of Chester. When the estuary silted up, Hoylake became the principle embarkation area for vessels bound for Ireland. Eventually, the pool silted and by the 1830s, a new channel was cut to Liverpool, marking the end of Hoylake as a port. The small fishing village of Hoose eventually grew into the seaside resort of Hoylake, and most of the village disappeared with the building of roads and new houses. *(Valentine's Series, posted 1911)*

Entrance to Hoylake.

Meols Drive and Market Street became the principle thoroughfares through the developing resort of Hoylake. Lined by shops and grand mansions built around the turn of the twentieth century, to the right we see Hoylake railway station and on the left Kings Gap which leads to the North Parade. *(The Wrench Series)*

Railway Station, Hoylake

Hoylake is served by two railway stations, Hoylake and Manor Road. Hoylake is a splendid Grade II listed art deco building and it replaced the station seen here (then a terminus station), which was opened in 1866 by the Hoylake Railway. Later, the line was taken over by the Hoylake & Birkenhead Rail & Tramway Company, and it became a through station when the line was extended to West Kirby in 1878. The line later became the property of the Seacombe, Hoylake & Deeside Railway and in 1891 the Wirral Railway. This Victorian building was replaced in 1938 shortly after the Mersey Railway and the LMS electrified the line. *(Valentine's Series)*

A view of the crossroads between Market Street and Shaw Street with the Punch Bowl Inn at the centre, seen here in the first decade of the twentieth century. Shaw Street was named after John Shaw who was the proprietor of the inn in 1840. *(Rajar Series)*

Church Street, like other streets at Hoylake, radiates from the promenade and has a number of grand Victorian mansions along it. The railway was instrumental in increasing the popularity of the area with summertime visitors arriving by train for weekend breaks by the seaside. Inevitably, for the well-to-do, Hoylake became a fashionable residential area for people from the crowded suburbs of Birkenhead and Liverpool, who were able to commute daily to the cities by the same railway. *(Post Office Hoylake, posted 1910)*

Market Street, Hoylake

Market Street, as its name suggests, is the main trading street and has an assortment of shops, pubs and restaurants. *(Valentine's Series)*

THE SHORE, HOYLAKE.

The sea walls and North Promenade built from local sandstone in the 1890s were always popular with Victorian and Edwardian gentle folk, taking a stroll in Sunday best clothes. The beach offered a similar opportunity for a stroll, although the tide when it was in would cover the entire beach. The sands at low water were a long way out, but bathers were able to use the nearby baths on the promenade. *(Clarendon Series, posted 1923)*

Promenade, Hoylake

Half way along the North Promenade is the Hoylake lifeboat station and launching slipway – one of the oldest on the British coast. It was founded by the Mersey Docks Committee on 18 September 1803 and the building seen here dates from 1899. The boat was launched from a carriage pulled by a team of horses a distance of up to 2 miles at low water – today a caterpillar tractor hauls the boat. A similar lifeboat station manned by the men of Hoylake was on Hilbre Island in the Dee Estuary; it had the advantage of a long slipway to launch the lifeboat at low water, and this station closed in 1938. The Hoylake lifeboat was taken over by the RNLI in 1894 and remains an important lifeboat station together with its sister station at Flint. The boats have been involved in many rescues of stricken vessels on the treacherous Dee sandbanks and frequently rescue people – sometimes from their vehicles – caught by the speed of the incoming tide. *(Valentine's Series)*

Yachts, Hoylake

The yachts seen here probably belong to members of the Hoylake Sailing Club, founded in 1887. The club is still going strong and members sail and race a similar type of clinker-built yacht. The yacht club stands next to the old lifeboat station in the previous postcard. *(The Waverley House Series, posted 1906)*

These rocks are on the eastern shore of the Hilbre group of islands and form part of the Dee Estuary Site of Special Scientific Interest. In the distance is the shoreline of Hoylake and West Kirby. The islands are a nature reserve used by thousands of over-wintering waders and wildfowl, and are a stopping-off point for migratory birds. The islands are also home to hundreds of Atlantic grey seals who like to bask on the sand banks off the west shore of the island when the tide is out. Hilbre is made up of three islands, the principle and the largest of which is Hilbre, the next largest island is Little Hilbre or Middle Eye and the smallest is Little Eye. (*Valentine's Series, posted 1942*)

The large Victorian house in the centre of this view, Telegraph House, was the home of the telegraph keeper and his family. The Trustees of Liverpool Docks established the telegraph signalling station in 1841 and the old telegraph station still survives and stands behind the building seen here. The telegraph station was part of a chain of similar signal stations used to relay messages between Holyhead and Liverpool, and ships at sea. An inn named the Seagull was established on the island to cater for the many visitors; it was run by a Joseph Hickson between 1790 and 1830 and part of the building is incorporated in Telegraph House. (*Publisher Unidentified*)

Promenade Hoylake, and Welsh Hills.

The North Promenade at Hoylake looking out across the Dee Estuary onto the Welsh hills which rise above Point of Ayr and Prestatyn. *(Hoylake Series)*

Red Rocks, Hoylake

It is at this point that the River Dee enters into the Irish Sea. Hilbre Point and these red sandstone rocks are at the very tip of the Wirral peninsula, jutting out into the Dee Estuary with the Irish Sea beyond. *(Hoylake Series, posted 1912)*